A Vegetarian Sampler

A kaleidoscope of styles and flavours for you to try with confidence and taste with pleasure.

A Vegetarian Sampler

Styles, Tastes, Occasions...
a Flavour of Each for You to Try

ALISON LEEMING

THORSONS PUBLISHING GROUP

First published 1988

Photography/Styling by Sue Atkinson, Mike Roles Studios

British Library Cataloguing in Publication Data

Leeming, Alison
A vegetarian sampler.
1. Vegetarian cookery
I. Title
641.5'636 TX837

ISBN 0-7225-1424-7

*Published by Thorsons Publishers Limited
Wellingborough, Northamptonshire,
NN8 2RQ England*

Printed in Great Britain

1 3 5 7 9 10 8 6 4 2

Contents

Introduction

This book is intended to be useful to the new vegetarian, established vegetarians, non-vegetarians and vegans. It aims to make clear that there exists a huge range of animal-free styles of cookery. Quick and simple meals for busy people, nutritious ideas for children, sweet things to bake, extravagant menus for entertaining and dishes that make use of the burgeoning 'strange' foods, such as sea vegetables, miso and tofu, as well as exotic fruits and vegetables and even flowers and herbs.

I have borne in mind, throughout, the questions raised time and time again in my cookery classes. I have attempted to demystify, debunk and generally make plain the ins and outs of vegetarianism, for dabbler and old hand alike.

I have also tried to convey my sense of enthusiasm and pleasure in cooking without meat. I love the sheer enormity of possibilities, the endless versatility of healthy, animal-free food—not to mention the comfort of knowing no-one had to die to feed me or mine. I hope my recipes give pleasure, provide sound information, and open new culinary horizons.

Vegetarianism and the appreciation of good food don't have to be mutually exclusive. The proof is in the eating, so all that remains is to begin.

HAPPY COOKING!

1.

Quick and Hearty Everyday Meals

The ideas contained in this chapter are given with the busy cook in mind. All the recipes are for four and it is a simple matter to convert the majority of them to vegan dishes by substituting bean milk, oil and tofu for the animal based products. Few and far between are those fortunates who have hours to spare in the kitchen. The recipes may contain ingredients with which you are not familiar—a glance through the Stocking Up section on page 80 should answer any queries you may have.

The secret of coping in a vegetarian kitchen is to combine sensible planning with a little imagination. Never be afraid to swap ingredients you are not so keen on for ones you know will go down well. When you are dead on your feet, or there isn't a second to spare for cooking, don't be afraid of turning to convenience foods—just choose them wisely to avoid too many additives and, if you can spare the time, add a little *je ne sais quoi* with spices or an imaginative topping to complement the packet or tin.

If you are new to vegetarian eating, take it slowly. The habits of a lifetime can't, and shouldn't, be changed overnight. No matter how keen or committed a person may be, a little respect for the digestive system is called for. Our systems adapt pretty quickly, but it is not fair or reasonable to zapp them with a high fibre diet when they have been used to puffy cereals and instant dessert for the last umpteen years! Cutting out white bread, full fat milk, salt and sugar must all be tackled in a slow and steady fashion. There are no instant solutions to healthy eating, in the same way there are no instant diets that work in the long term. It simply comes down to spending time re-educating your body to new eating patterns.

Change from full fat milk to skimmed milk over a goodly period to allow the taste buds to adjust. Go for semi-skimmed milk first, then, only when you are fully adapted should you go on to try skimmed. It may take several months to educate your palate to happily and naturally reject the foods that have contributed to putting Britons at the top of the heart attack league. Daunting? No, not really. You will be astonished at how the change comes about! I repeat though, make your changes slowly and follow the NACNE recommendations on cutting down fat, sugar and salt, and increasing fibre. Don't worry overmuch about protein. Deficiency is not very likely. Don't go mad stuffing yourself and loved ones with beans and nuts—you'll only get fat! There is every reason to believe that the government recommended daily protein intake of 2–3 oz (55–85 grams) for adults may be reduced as greater knowledge is gained.

If different members of your family demand special meals, then I would be inclined to tell them to think again. It is easier on the cook to prepare one meal. Dissenters can have bread and cheese on the day(s) it is not their turn to dictate the main dish of the day—or they could, of course, cook their own. I honestly feel that expecting the cook to prepare two or three main courses for every meal is not reasonable. Rotating meals so that everyone can expect to have a meal they approve of at least a few times a week is a much more reasonable and practical approach.

Three Tips for Happier Cooking

1. Buy in three or four bags of favourite beans. I like chick peas, black-eyed beans, red kidney beans and flageolets. The numbers of bags should depend on how many good sized pans you have. Before you go to bed, tip each variety of bean into its own large pan. Cover well with cold water and retire, with a good book, to a warm and comfortable bed. Next day, pour away the soaking water, cover the beans with ample quantities of fresh cold water, bring the pans to the boil and simmer for anything from 30 minutes to an hour, until they are soft but not disintegrated. Add a strip of kombu (see Stocking Up on page 84) to each pan at the start of cooking. This helps soften the beans as well as adding valuable minerals and trace elements. If your beans take forever to cook, they are old—buy them somewhere else next time! When the beans have cooled, bag them in portions suitable for your household and put them in the freezer. I use those plastic bags on a roll. Don't forget to label them. I often get a bag of beans out of the freezer in the morning, without any idea what I will do with them in the evening. Inspiration never fails, even if it's only a quick tomato sauce to stir the beans into, with a heap of noodles to go beneath and a generous dollop of yogurt to top it off. My bean bags may turn into a vegetable pie with a pastry or mashed potato topping, or a simple bean curry, courtesy of a jar of curry paste, or a quick main course salad with olives, avocado, tomatoes and fresh green beans and a huge lump of crispy hot garlic bread. The possibilities are endless once you have come to terms with the bewilderment that changing your diet can cause. Cooking with beans does not have to mean endless hours in the kitchen.

Some types of beans, such as red kidney beans, need to be boiled for ten minutes before they are brought to a simmer.

2. Season food with fresh lemon juice or cider vinegar instead of salt. A teaspoon or two of lemon juice or vinegar is a lot more effective than any amount of herbs when it comes to salt replacements. It is, on the whole, a much better idea to educate the taste buds away from salt than to train them to become independent on proprietary salt replacements. If your family refuse to relinquish the salt pot from the table, buy a new pot with the smallest hole you can find and use that instead. Don't tell *them*, but studies have shown that people use less salt without noticing, when fooled in this beneficial way! Alternatively you could put the salt in a bowl (if

it absolutely must go on the table), and leave them to pick it up by the pinch — no salt spoons— another ruse to help cut consumption. I also use the odd pinch of sugar (in savoury dishes) to bring out flavours. It really works, and I see no harm if the overall diet is fairly low in sugar. Herbs do, of course, have their place, but they add their own flavour rather than enhancing what is already there.

3. When you have had enough of the kitchen sink, and the siren voice of 'Woman's Hour' calls, try my highly-recommended new approach to your kitchen cupboards. First you need a handful of raw, unsoaked aduki beans. Grind them to a fine powder in the coffee mill and store the ground beans in a screw top jar. Second, buy a bottle of sesame oil. It is fairly readily available in Chinese, Indian, Greek or Turkish shops, and lots of health food stores now stock the unrefined oil too. Only buy the kind that is a deepish, sludgy brown colour with a wonderfully powerful sesame smell—what is the point of a product that has had all its best qualities refined out of it?

Take a generous teaspoon (5ml) of the aduki grindings cupped in your palm. Moisten with a little warm water to make a paste. Use the paste to give your face and throat a gentle, but thorough scrub. Rinse away the grindings with lashings of cold water. Repeat this every day for a week and you will acquire the most beautifully fresh complexion. If you carry out the face scrub just before a bath, follow it with a thin coat of sesame oil. Tissue it off after the bath and your skin will positively glow! To encourage your hair to match the glowing complexion, rub 2 tablespoons (30ml) of sesame oil well into the scalp and hair and wrap in an old scarf at least one hour before shampooing as normal. To lounge in a hot bathroom, enveloped in the powerful scent of sesame oil, listening to the dulcet tones of 'Woman's Hour' can feel like joy unbounded— simple soul that I am! I'd recommend this alternative approach to the kitchen cupboards to any weary cook.

Chick Pea Hot Pot

Use a bag of frozen chick peas or a tin (rinse away the sugary, salty water) for a really speedy meal. I like this best with plain boiled potatoes, better still with baked potatoes if there is time to cook them, and a green vegetable like spinach or plain salad. Fry a couple of onions, a green pepper and a tablespoon of ground coriander in a touch of oil before adding the mushroom mixture for a totally different effect.

8 oz (225g) large mushrooms
1 lb (455g) cooked chick peas
2 tablespoons (30ml) soy sauce
5 oz (140g) smetana or sour cream or thick yogurt
2 teaspoons (10ml) miso

Wash and roughly chop the mushrooms. Put them in a large pan with the chick peas and soy sauce. Bring gently to the boil—the juice will soon start to run from the mushrooms. Turn the heat full on and boil the mixture rapidly until almost no liquid remains. Stir in the smetana, sour cream or yogurt and miso and gently reheat. Do not boil again or the beneficial enzymes in the miso will be destroyed.

The cold mixture makes a very good base for a main course salad if you add cucumber, tomatoes, celery, sweetcorn kernels and red peppers, or whatever else you have to hand. Serve the salad with chunks of granary or garlic bread to set the taste buds tingling.

Creamed Flageolets with Sesame Seeds

Use frozen, home-cooked beans or tinned, just like the previous recipe, for a splendid quickie hot pot. Transform the mixture into a pie by topping it with a crust of ready made pastry for those in a hurry or home-made wholemeal for those with a little more time (recipe on page 44). Serve the Creamed Flageolets with potatoes and vegetables. If you don't like onions, use celery instead. Don't serve potatoes if there is a pie crust—no need for too much carbohydrate!

3 large onions
2 tablespoons (30ml) oil
3 tablespoons (45ml) plain flour
¾ pint (425ml) milk
1 lb (455g) cooked flageolets
1 teaspoon (5ml) cider vinegar
3 oz (85g) sesame seeds

Peel and thinly slice the onions. Fry them in oil until deeply browned. Sprinkle over the flour and continue to cook for a further two minutes. Add the milk, stir well, bring to the boil and cook until thick, then add the beans. Season with vinegar.

In a separate small pan, cook the sesame seeds over a low heat until they are brown—stir them often. No oil is needed, but beware as the seeds can appear unchanged for what seems like ages (3 or 4 minutes) and then they are suddenly browned. Don't let them burn. Stir the seeds into the creamed beans and serve, or pour into a pie dish, add a crust and bake until crisp and golden.

Bodington Bake

Serve this easy to prepare lentil bake with a salad or green vegetables for a meal that is bursting with goodness. You can vary the flavour by changing the cheese—a mixture of Parmesan and Emmental is good. Try different herbs or swap the tomato purée for a tablespoon of naturally brewed soy sauce.

6 oz (170g) continental lentils
1 medium onion
4 oz (115g) mature cheddar cheese
1 tablespoon (15ml) oil
1 tablespoon (15ml) tomato purée
1 teaspoon (5ml) dried basil or mixed herbs
2 eggs
black pepper

Cook the lentils until tender. Continental lentils don't need soaking and cook in 20–30 minutes. Fry the finely chopped onion in oil until soft. Add the drained lentils to the fried onion and stir in the rest of the ingredients. Mix well together.

Lightly grease a deep dish and pile in the mixture. Cover with foil and bake for one hour at 375°F/190°C (gas mark 5). Remove the foil covering for the last quarter of an hour to allow the Bodington Bake to brown. It tastes splendid hot or cold and is excellent for buffets, especially if cooked in a loaf tin for easy slicing later.

Instant Cheese Sauce

This sauce is so good it is worthy of the most elegant dinner party. It is also so ludicrously simple that it is appropriate for this quick meals chapter. Serve it over boiled or jacket potatoes accompanied by lots of fresh vegetables as an everyday standby. Pour it over freshly made fettucine and top with chervil or chives and offer a salad of red radicchio and curly endive with a hazelnut oil dressing for a grand occasion. As it is made with Brie, one of the lower fat cheeses, it is not as unhealthy as one might think.

8 oz (225g) Brie
5 oz (140g) yogurt
1 oz (30g) butter—optional

Remove the rind and cut the cheese into pieces. Put the roughly chopped cheese into a small pan with the butter (if you are using it), and melt together over a very low heat. If the cheese boils it will become stringy and nasty, so don't hurry it. When the cheese is melted, stir in the pot of yogurt and continue gently heating. Again, the mixture must not boil. Serve over pasta or potatoes.

Nutty Loaf

Another simple bake for everyday meals. Try using walnuts or almonds for a change. A salad of tomatoes and green beans or lightly steamed carrots and cabbage would go equally well with the loaf, hot or cold. Potatoes are unnecessary as the bake contains breadcrumbs. Serve a tomato sauce, miso gravy or simply a spoonful of chutney to accompany it.

8 oz (225g) fresh peanuts
6 oz (170g) fresh wholemeal breadcrumbs
2 oz (55g) porridge oats
2 tablespoons (30ml) peanut butter
3 tablespoons (45ml) olive oil
1 x 15 oz (425g) tin tomatoes
1 teaspoon (5ml) dried thyme
½ teaspoon (2.5ml) dried sage
pinch cayenne pepper
1 teaspoon (5ml) vinegar
pinch sugar

Chop the nuts roughly. If you use a blender, be careful not to reduce them too finely. Mix the breadcrumbs, porridge oats, peanut butter and oil to make a crumbly mixture. Drain the tomatoes, and mix them with the chopped nuts, thyme, sage, cayenne pepper, vinegar and sugar.

Spread two thirds of the crumble mixture into a lightly greased dish. Put the nut and tomato mixture on top and cover that with the remaining crumble. Bake for 30 minutes at 400°F/200°C (gas mark 6).

Spiced Beans

Another candidate for the bags of beans from the freezer, or you could use tinned, of course (remember to rinse them!). I like butter or haricot beans in this recipe, but black-eyed beans, chick peas or red beans are just as suitable. Serve generously topped with yogurt, accompanied by boiled rice, hot pitta bread or a jacket potato. Leftovers make excellent rissoles if you bulk out the mixture with plenty of breadcrumbs before shaping, egging, crumbing and frying. The rissoles are good with a plain tomato sauce and green vegetables.

1 tablespoon (15ml) oil
1 teaspoon (5ml) curry paste (use a hottish one)
¾ lb (340g) beans of your choice
2 teaspoons (10ml) sweet chutney or marmalade
11 oz (300g) tin sweetcorn kernels
8 oz (225g) broad beans—frozen, tinned or fresh

Fry the curry paste in the oil for a minute, then add the rest of the ingredients together with just enough water to moisten them—roughly a scant ¼ pint (140ml). Bring to the boil and simmer for a minute to allow the beans to heat through before serving. You could embellish the sauce with garlic, fresh ginger or any other spices.

Aubergine and Red Bean Sauce for Pasta

This is the last of the frozen or tinned bean recipes in this chapter. The 'secret' ingredient in this thick, rich sauce is the cider vinegar, which brings up the flavour beautifully. Don't stint the garlic or oil. Serve the sauce over fresh or dried spaghetti, fettucine or macaroni, with a crisp salad. A topping of Parmesan or Geska (see Stocking Up on page 82) is pleasant.

3 medium onions
4-6 cloves garlic
3-4 tablespoons (45-60ml) oil
1 tablespoon (15ml) ground coriander
1 large aubergine
15 oz (340g) tin tomatoes
2 tablespoons (30ml) tomato purée
8 oz (225g) roughly mashed red beans
2 teaspoons (10ml) cider vinegar

Finely chop the onions and garlic and fry with the coriander until soft. Add the aubergine chopped into small cubes, the tinned tomatoes including their juice, the tomato purée and ¼ pint (140ml) water. Boil for 20-30 minutes until the aubergine is tender. Add the roughly mashed beans and allow them to heat through. The sauce will be thick and rich. Season with cider vinegar and serve over the pasta of your choice.

Avocado and Macaroni Quickie

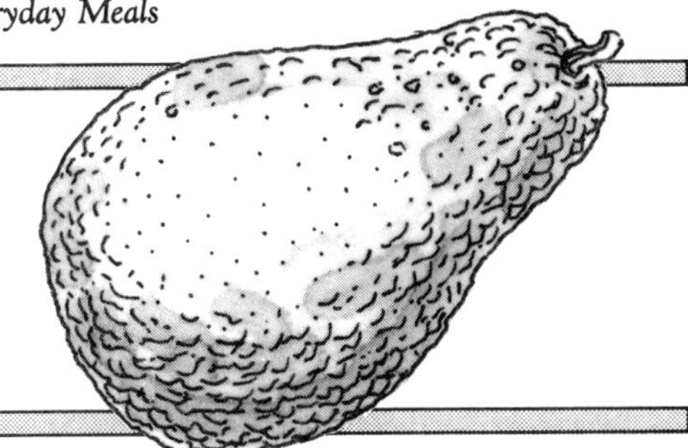

Use Hass avocados, the ones with the nubbly, dark purply brown skins, for the best flavour. Avocados are rich in protein and are very high in monosaturated oils. They are also rich in B vitamins and folic acid as well as vitamin E, making them an excellent food, particularly for women. It is time to stop thinking of them as fattening and start concentrating on their astonishingly healthy properties. (Provided they haven't been irradiated, of course!)

12 oz (340g) wholemeal macaroni
12 oz (340g) mushrooms
1 tablespoon (15ml) oil
8 oz (225g) green beans—fresh or frozen
3 tablespoons (45ml) soy sauce
3 avocados

Cook the macaroni in plenty of boiling water until *al dente*, then drain well. Wipe and roughly chop the mushrooms and fry them in a tablespoon of oil for 2 or 3 minutes. Add the green beans and soy sauce and boil the contents of the pan fiercely until most of the moisture has boiled away.

Add the drained macaroni and fairly finely chopped avocado and allow to heat through for a few minutes before serving. The avocado should be merely warmed—if it gets too hot and starts to cook, the flavour will change dramatically, becoming unpleasantly bitter.

Serve with a plain tomato and cucumber salad and a generous spoonful of mild, whole grain mustard.

Simple Summer Instant Meal

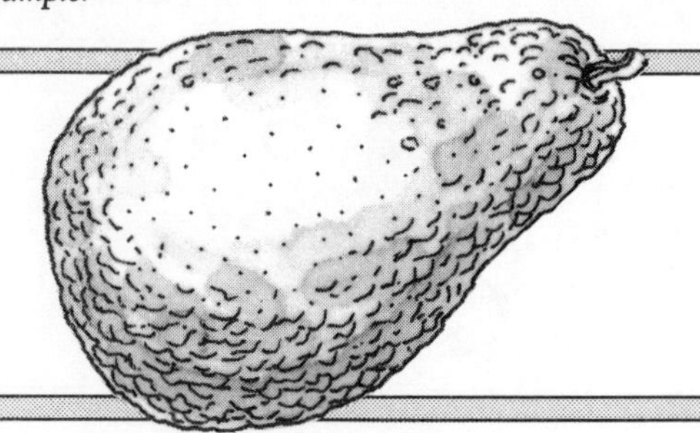

Here is an almost 'no cook' meal, that will revive the most jaded palate on a warm summer evening, especially when eaten in the garden with a glass or two of chilled white wine! It is not so much a recipe, more a collection of ingredients.

2 lb (900g) tiny new potatoes
2 avocados
2 'beef' tomatoes
6 oz (170g) black olives—preferably Calamata
4 tablespoons (60ml) capers
juice of ½ lemon
1 tablespoon (15ml) oil
5 oz (140g) sour cream
pinch chilli pepper
1 clove garlic

Wash the potatoes and boil or steam until cooked. Peel and slice the avocados, laying a fan of slices on each plate. Chop the tomatoes into chunky pieces and toss them with the capers and olives. Pile a little salad on each plate.

Mix the oil and lemon together, and pour over the avocado, leaving the tomato salad undressed for a nice contrast of sharp, fresh flavours. Beat the sour cream, chilli and crushed garlic together. Pour a dribble of cream over the avocados so they are now double dressed, and make a puddle on the plate for the 'Greek warm' new potatoes to be dipped in. The contrast of tastes, textures and dressings is sublime.

Baked Stuffed Aubergines

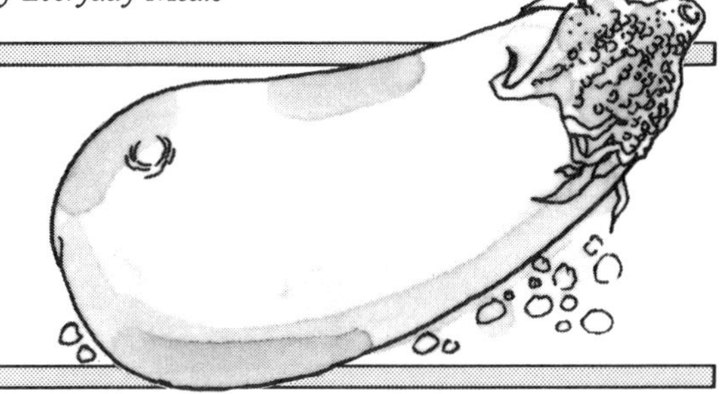

Aubergines don't need salting anymore and I simply can't understand why so many cookery books still insist it should be done. The people who engineer our fruit and vegetables are to be congratulated (well, just this once!) for doing the right thing. They have bred out the old bitterness without ruining the flavour, as seems to have happened with so much else. Serve this dish with salad or fresh vegetables. The breadcrumbs make potatoes unnecessary.

2 good sized aubergines
2–3 tablespoons (30–45ml) oil
3 large onions
3–4 cloves garlic
1 large green pepper
3 tablespoons (45ml) tomato purée
½ pint (285ml) red wine, stock or water
2 teaspoons (10ml) oregano
3 oz (85g) sunflower seeds or pine kernels
4–5 oz (115g–140g) fresh brown breadcrumbs
4 tablespoons (60ml) Parmesan or Geska

Slice the aubergines in half along their length, scoop out the flesh and rub the shells generously, inside and out, with oil. Put the finely chopped onions, chopped garlic, chopped green pepper, tomato purée, wine and oregano in a pan together with the chopped aubergine flesh. Bring to the boil and simmer for 20–30 minutes.

When the sauce is cooked, stir in the seeds, breadcrumbs and Parmesan or Geska. The breadcrumbs will soak up most of the moisture. Pile the mixture into the oiled aubergine shells and set them in a shallow dish to which you have added 3–4 tablespoons (40–60ml) of water. Cover with foil and bake in a fairly hot oven 400°F/200°C (gas mark 6) for 30–40 minutes.

Stuffed aubergines are as good hot or cold. If there isn't time to bake the aubergines, serve the filling without bothering with the baking stage.

Savoury Westmorland Loaf

This is one of my mother's specialities. I have adapted her original recipe to use Sosmix, a vegetable alternative to sausage meat. This loaf is quick and easy, and ideal for newcomers to vegetarianism longing for something familiar, but nevertheless animal-free. Serve it with crisply roast potatoes and parsnips, sprouts, carrots, apple sauce and rich gravy.

175g packet *Sosmix*
6 oz (170g) cooking apples
6 oz (170g) onions
1 teaspoon (5ml) sage
2 teaspoons (10ml) thyme
1 egg

Put the *Sosmix* in a large bowl and stir in ½ pint (285ml) water. Peel and finely chop the apple and onions. Add them to the *Sosmix* together with the herbs and egg. Mix everything together. Pile into a loaf tin and bake at 375°F/190°C (gas mark 5) for 30–35 minutes. Allow it to cool a little to make it easier to slice at the table. Leftovers make a good sandwich filling or cold slices can be served with salad.

2.
Children's Treats

Feeding children can often present problems. Tiny appetities, stubborn ways and an unhealthy interest in sweets and crisps combine to worry many parents. Making a battle of meal times is pointless. Children are incredibly strong willed and, in the final analysis, usually win! Avoid battles at all costs. An unhappy child (or adult for that matter!) can't be expected to have a good appetite. Meal times should be a pleasant occasion to catch up on family doings when everyone sits down to the table together. Remember, above all, that what may look like a tiny amount of food to an adult can be quite a lot for a child's small stomach. A high fibre diet can be dauntingly bulky for a small child, so a little care and planning is called for. If a complete meal is out of the question, it is better to accept a child's decision and get round the problem by offering frequent nutritious snacks. It is not so much a matter of quantity, the important element is the quality of the food we give our children. Fussing, worrying and fighting over food will simply ensure that all the parties involved are miserable. As a rule, most children will eat enough food to keep themselves well nourished, despite what worried parents may feel. It is only in exceptional circumstances that some children will require special help and then nutrition experts should be called in.

This chapter gives a selection of practical ideas for nutritious treats for small people. I think it is worth giving a brief guide to the basic principles of nutrition to help with making sound choices about what children should eat.

Proteins

Proteins have two basic tasks. One is to promote growth, the other is to repair and maintain the body. Bearing these functions in mind, it becomes easy to understand that growing children require only a little less protein than adults, whose requirements are currently thought to be around 2–3 ounces (55–85 grams) per day. Children's needs vary from ¾ oz (20g) when very young, building to almost the same levels as adults by the time they enter their teens. Having given the hard facts, I wouldn't want anyone to get into a spin about protein consumption. There is no need at all to worry about the protein levels in a reasonable diet—so don't! In fact, if anything, we over-fed Westerners are eating far more protein than is good for us. Provided your child has enough energy to play and drive you to alternate bouts of distraction and joy, you can rest assured that protein consumption is not a problem. If you have a child who is difficult to coax to eating, then 'quality not quantity' should become your motto. Anxious hours spent totting up calories and grams of protein or battling over pudding *after* greens is generally neither productive nor necessary. If pudding is all that will be eaten, accept the inevitable; but ensure that it is a high protein, healthy pudding rather than a dish of empty-caloried, additive-laced, plastic food.

Sugars

Sugars, which are included in the carbohydrate group, are important for energy. But sugar leads to rotten teeth and excess weight. Hidden sugar (as well as fats) in so many processed foods can often be held responsible for over-plump children. It is not only unwise, it is virtually impossible to cut sugar completely out of children's diets. From their earliest days they are conditioned to sweetness, one only has to think about how sweet human milk is! The point is to offer sweetness in its whole form, such as carrots, raisins or bananas, rather than in a refined and processed sweet drink or chocolate bar. Sugars give only 'empty calories', so called because they contain no vitamins, no minerals, no protein and no fibre, in fact nothing at all that will benefit a growing body. Even molasses, the most unrefined of the sugars, contains 95 per cent sugar and only 5 per cent of anything that is nutritionally useful. Save refined sugary things for very special treats, and rely on fresh and dried fruits and nuts for everyday eating, attempting to cultivate a savoury rather than a sweet tooth.

Fats

Saturated fat in excess will lead to problems later in life and must be kept to a minimum in a child's diet. It is worth pointing out that in the vegetable world, coconut and palm oil are saturated fats and as such they must be used sparingly. We hear much about increasing poly-unsaturates in the diet. For myself, I prefer mono-unsaturated oils: olive oil and peanut/groundnut oil for everyday use, hazelnut and walnut oils for special occasions. I avoid all margarines, most of which are rich only in saturated fats, water and 'E' numbers. If you do give your children vegetable margarines, look out for 'hydrogenation' or a similar term on the label. A poly-unsaturate becomes a saturate once it has been subjected to this process. I also use unsalted butter, albeit sparingly, to bake with. I feel sure that the current mania for poly-unsaturates is not particularly healthy—anything, poly-unsaturates included, consumed to excess, most especially by children, is not wise. I think the English habit of spreading butter on bread, crackers and buns is unnecessary as well as unhealthy, and children really don't miss it. We would do well to adopt the ways of our European cousins who rarely use either butter or margarine.

The fat in **milk** remains a vexed and controversial question. As a general guide, children under two should be given whole milk, children between two and five can be given semi-skimmed milk, and over fives, skimmed. But this will depend on how well-nourished a child is. Faddy eaters will need all the nourishment you can persuade them to consume and therefore whole milk at any age, under such circumstances, is best. Certainly, by the age of five, skimmed milk is suitable for the average well-nourished child. There are those who feel that after the age of three, skimmed or semi-skimmed milk is to be preferred. It is for you to decide whether your child is merely taking milk as a thirst quencher, in which case low fat is best, or whether it is a valuable part of the diet in which case whole milk is best. In terms of protein, whole, skimmed and semi-skimmed milk are virtually identical. Calcium levels are highest in skimmed milk, slightly less in semi-skimmed and lowest in whole milk, but the differences are small. Vitamin A is fat soluble so is removed in the skimming process (though in some skimmed and semi-skimmed milks, the vitamins are returned after processing). B vitamins are unaffected by removal of the fat and are, like calcium, somewhat greater in semi-skimmed and skimmed milk.

A good foundation of healthy eating habits established in childhood is probably the best legacy a parent can pass on to a child. Saturated fats are one of the major causes of heart disease, and one which parents could do so much to help their children avoid in later life.

Fibre

Fibre plays a vital role in healthy eating. There is little I can say here that hasn't been said before, except that children should not be given refined bran which can affect the body's absorption of nutrients. Fruit and vegetables are high in fibre and there should be no need for refined fibre in a diet rich in fresh produce. If the dreaded constipation is a problem, then a bowl of porridge or a few oat cookies or a dish of stewed apricots and figs, an extra slice of wholemeal toast, or high fibre vegetables like corn cobs or spinach would be better than doses of artificial laxatives. Remember that a fibrous and therefore a bulky diet can cause problems for small appetites, filling them up before they have consumed enough nourishment for a growing body. Concentrate on foods that do not take up too much stomach space and have a high ratio of nutrients to bulk. Tofu is the perfect example of a low bulk, high protein food.

Vitamins and Minerals

Vitamins, minerals and trace elements will be plentiful in a diet full of fresh produce. It is worth working at getting children to eat as much fresh fruit and vegetables as possible in order to keep up good stocks of vitamins and minerals. There is growing evidence that poor nutrition adversely affects intelligence. Zinc, a mineral trace element, is vital for growth and affects appetite. Recent studies into allergy syndromes have established that a significant proportion of sufferers have very low zinc levels. Sesame seeds contain exceptionally high levels of zinc, and most other seeds contain generous amounts. A diet rich in trace elements, minerals and vitamins is the answer to many health problems. But bear in mind that irradiation destroys almost all the vitamins present in fresh food as well as altering previously beneficial oils.

Additives

Additives are a problem in children's diet, though thankfully things are improving dramatically. Manufacturers have been forced, due to consumer pressure, to offer an increasing range of products minus the worst additives, and some items can now be purchased that are completely additive free.

Additives have been found to be responsible for a wide range of illnesses including asthma, urticaria, migraine and hyperactivity. Abdominal pains, diarrhoea and aching limbs as well as inability to sleep and persistent night cough have all been laid at the door of additives. Colourings (E100–E180) and preservatives (E200–E321) are acknowledged to be the most common causes of intolerance. If you suspect that your child may be suffering from an allergy, then professional advice is essential. Your doctor should be able to put you in touch with support groups in your area as well as offering sound advice on how to cope with what is, at long last, coming to be acknowledged as a very real problem. It seems to me utterly shocking that for so long parents have had to put up with the inference that they were to blame for 'unruly' and 'ill-disciplined' offspring, rather than the nasty and unwholesome chemicals added to nasty and unwholesome items masquerading as food. It is acknowledged that children are most susceptible to additives, and should therefore consume less than adults, but they do, in fact, consume far higher quantities than us. The average adult consumes about twice the 'acceptable' daily intake, the average child about five times this level. Ninety-three per cent of additives have no nutritional value and ninety per cent are flavourings. Some products simply wouldn't be eaten if our taste buds weren't deceived by flavourings. Do our children really need additives that are estimated to induce hyperactivity in around ten per cent of them? Ten per cent represents a huge number of children, and what of their families, burdened with coping? All in the name of progress and profit. Though matters are undoubtedly improving, there remains a long way still to go. As a general rule, if you buy processed foods (and who doesn't?), read the label and try to avoid buying products that contain E numbers in the ranges E100–E180 and E200–E321. Food colourings seem to be almost unavoidable when it comes to something like birthday cakes. A decoration on a brown and white theme—buttercream and chocolate or carob buttons—may not be a dazzling multi-coloured extravaganza, but it is certainly a lot less hazardous! You could always add a little extra colour with non-edible decorations like fancy candle holders, small toys or even coloured ribbons. The government bans the use of some additives in food products intended for babies and young children. But the obvious point that young children eat a huge variety of foods not designed exclusively for them is not legislated for. There are indeed some additives that are useful and beneficial, but on the whole they are best avoided—when in doubt, leave them out! It is interesting to note that most of the food industry takes the exactly opposite view—where there's doubt, pile them in. Humans give birth to children, not guinea pigs, I say!

Some useful addresses are:

The Hyperactive Children's Support Group
Mayfield House
Barnham, Bognor Regis
West Sussex PO22 0BJ

Action Against Allergy
43 The Downs
London SW20 8HG

The National Society for Research into Allergy
PO Box 291
London N5 1DU
(send large s.a.e. & 50p)

Elephant's Breath

If your child is refusing to eat anything but pudding, this dish, bursting with protein and vitamins, is the perfect solution. Make a pretence of requiring the savoury course to be eaten—as usual—but give in, not too swiftly, and present the pudding with an air bordering on resignation. If you are too eager, the average highly suspicious child will smell a rat (so to speak) and your healthy eating plans will come to nought. Silken tofu is high in protein and very high in calcium (containing even more than the firm varieties) so it's ideal for growing bodies. The iron in the dried apricots makes a valuable contribution too. Toasted almonds are another protein food, but you can omit them if you prefer. This dish is virtually a meal in itself, and is suitable for piling into a small container and adding to a packed lunch. It is also (without the nuts) an excellent early solid for babies and a calcium booster for pregnant, lactating and menopausal women. Could anyone ask for more from one simple dish?

4 oz (115g) whole almonds
8 oz (225g) silken tofu
4 oz (115g) dried apricots
1 teaspoon (5ml) cinnamon
2 egg whites
honey to taste

Toast the almonds by placing them in a single layer on a dish and baking them in a moderate oven for 5 minutes. There is no need to skin them. Place all the other ingredients except the egg whites in a blender and process for 2 or 3 minutes until smooth. The matter of the honey I leave to your discretion, but remember that less is best with all sugars—even honey. There is no need to soak the apricots unless they are very hard.

Whisk the egg whites until stiff and peaky, then fold them into the apricot and tofu cream. I like the nuts to be quite chunky, so I usually put them in a plastic bag and hit them a few times with a rolling pin to break them up a little before stirring them into the cream. You could whizz them in the blender with the rest of the ingredients for a fairly finely chopped effect, or grind them in the coffee/nut mill for a really smooth texture. The choice is yours.

Serve chilled or at room temperature with a few slivers of apple or a small biscuit for a crisp contrast. Elephant's Breath looks surprisingly good in elegant stemmed glasses set on doily covered plates, and accompanied by *langue de chat* biscuits for a very grown up dessert, especially when made with hazelnuts or pecans —nothing if not versatile!

Banana and Chocolate Chip 'Ice-Cream'

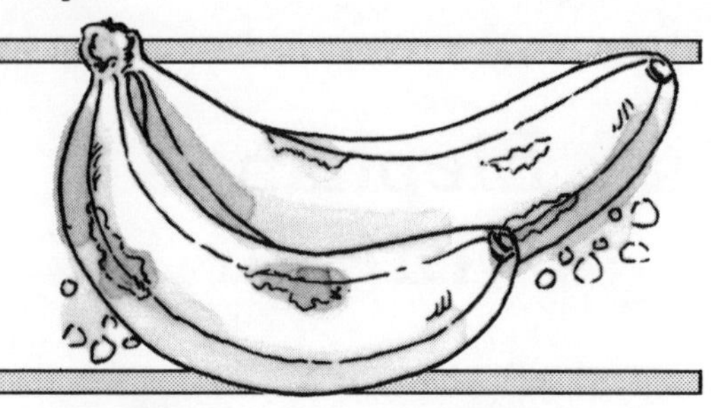

Another tofu treat full of protein and calcium, with the banana adding B vitamins for healthy skin, nerves and general growth. Chocolate is one of those items that some children must not eat, that many parents disapprove of and that the majority of children adore. Use carob if you have a child suffering from allergy to chocolate, or simply if you prefer. Under most circumstances however, I believe that a little chocolate, despite its fat, sugar and buzz-inducing theobromine, isn't too bad in moderation. Carob is less sugary and is sometimes lower in fat, though many bars contain palm and/or coconut fats which are high in saturates and therefore not particularly to be recommended. Some carob bars are made with bean milk and are a boon for parents struggling to cope with a milk-free diet. For such a diet, this is an entirely dairy-free ice cream if made with a bean milk carob bar. For those fortunates who need not take such matters into consideration, it is simply a delicious, low-fat treat. This ice, like any real ice, tends to set quite hard in the freezer—no 'soft scoop' chemical concoction here! Allow it to soften for 10 minutes or so in the fridge before serving. Once you understand the basic idea, the combinations are endless. Try any fresh or dried fruit, nuts or seeds. A cooling ice to lubricate sore throats, easily digested by invalids and greatly relished at rumbustious birthday parties for a healthy alternative to those additive-packed mixtures in plastic tubs, pretending to be ice-cream.

4 oz (115g) chocolate—plain, milk or carob
8 oz (225g) silken tofu
3 ripe bananas
honey to taste

Place the chocolate in the freezer for 10 minutes to become really hard. The more ripe the bananas, the less honey will be needed. Place all the ingredients, except the chocolate, into a blender goblet and process until smooth. Grate the well chilled chocolate and stir it into the banana mix.

Freeze until fairly firm then, using an ice-cream scoop, place individual portions onto a baking sheet and return to the freezer for its final hardening. When the portions are completely frozen, store them in a plastic bag or carton. If they are stuck to the tray, hold it over your next available pan of boiling potatoes or whatever, for a minute or two. This will soon loosen them. Remember to soften in the fridge before serving.

Cheesy Tractor Wheels

This is a simple idea which takes full account of children's sensibilities. First is the fantasy element. A gourmet may feel that food should be splendidly presented with a title that gives a clear idea of the ingredients. Not so with children. Presentation should indeed have some thought behind it, but who can deny that a child will tuck into a 'Tractor Wheel' with a lot more relish than a plain old boring sandwich. They can also be very wary of a sandwich filling, spending more time dismantling the thing than consuming it—if indeed they do at all. Miso, which is in the recipe, is a soya bean product. It is similar to yeast extract, but not so salty and with a much less overpowering taste. I now use it for all purposes where I would previously have used yeast extract. It makes marvellous stock and is rich in protein, calcium, iron and vitamins including B_{12}*. A few Tractor Wheels with a little spinach and/or freshly grated carrot make a very acceptable meal. The bread, preferably wholemeal, should be very fresh to enable it to roll up easily. If your children will only eat white bread, it is worth trying to buy Greek or Italian white bread, if that is at all possible, because it is made with a less refined flour than English white bread flour.*

Per slice of bread
(preferably wholemeal):
1 teaspoon (5ml) miso
1 oz (30g) grated Cheddar or Edam cheese
1 teaspoon (5ml) olive oil

Cut the crusts from the bread and spread one side with miso. The habit of spreading bread with butter or margarine is one that should be avoided. If a filling is wet and likely to make the bread soggy, a much more health conscious approach would be to put the wet item between a lettuce leaf barrier. This has the same effect as butter in stopping the wetness getting into the bread, but the saturated fat is drastically reduced, if not cut out all together.

Sprinkle the cheese over the miso then roll the bread into a fat sausage. Wrap tightly in tin foil and refrigerate for 10–30 minutes, to help prevent them unrolling. Slice the roll into ½ inch (1 cm) wheels—after the manner of slicing up a swiss roll. Use the oil to very lightly grease a baking tray and lay the wheels on it, sprinkling the last of the oil over the top of the wheels just before they go into a hot oven 425°F/220°C (gas mark 7). Secure the wheels with cocktail sticks if there still seems to be any danger of them unwrapping. Bake or grill until crisp.

The wheels are as good cold as hot and make a pleasant addition to a lunch box. If you intend to make a large batch of Tractor Wheels, it is best to slice the loaf along its length, rolling the slice up sideways. In this way you can prepare a large number of wheels very quickly. They are also pretty acceptable with a glass of red wine—especially if you spice them up with a touch of cayenne and grated nutmeg.....cook's perks?

Magpie Nests

Potatoes are a valuable source of vitamin C, more because we eat so many of them, than because they are high in vitamin C. This quick and easy combination of grated carrot and potato is a handy way of getting children to eat carrots and boost supplies of sight improving vitamin A. I use peanut oil, also known as groundnut oil, for general frying— (see Stocking Up on page 82). Arame is a sea vegetable and it is time that we used more of these delicious and highly nutritious foods. There are many varieties of sea vegetable, arame being one of the best introductions because of its mild flavour. It contains good supplies of protein, calcium, iodine, potassium and iron. Ounce for ounce, it contains very much higher levels of protein and calcium than cow's milk, and, of course, no fat.

¼ oz (7g) arame
2 medium-sized potatoes
2 medium-sized carrots
oil for shallow frying

Arame usually comes in packets weighing about 1¾ oz (50g). There is little point in trying to weigh out ¼ oz (7g)—you don't need to be so very precise anyway—so judge what you think is barely one fifth of the packet and pull out that much. Pop it into a bowl and cover it with about ½ pint (285ml) cold water. Leave it to soak while you prepare the vegetables.

Wash and scrub them well to remove as much of the pesticides and sprouting inhibitors as possible. Some believe this is a waste of time as the chemicals penetrate deeply into fruit and vegetables, but scrubbing at least makes me feel better! Buying organically grown produce is the only genuine answer. Peel the carrots and grate them. I leave the skin on organic potatoes: its extra fibre, tastes good and the vitamins lie just beneath the skin, so peeling diminishes their nutritional value. Grate the potatoes and mix them with the grated carrot.

Squeeze as much water as possible from the arame and add it to the mixture. Don't throw away the soaking water. It contains some of the seaweed nutrients, so use it to water your plants, or save it to be added to soups and stocks, or pour it into your pet's feeding bowl for a mineral rich health booster. Budgies like it too!

The mixture of grated vegetables should be shallow fried, over a medium to slow heat, in tablespoon-sized 'nests', until crisply browned. You could fry smaller or larger amounts depending on the appetites you are catering for. Squash the mixture fairly well down once it is in the pan to help it stick together. A few drops of shoyu (a fancy name for natural soy sauce) on top and a spoonful or two of cottage cheese liberally sprinkled with sunflower seeds makes a splendid meal for any Magpie enthusiast.

Avocado Crispies

1 slice wholemeal bread
¼-½ ripe avocado
1 scant tablespoon (15 ml) lemon juice

These little toasty triangles spread with mashed avocado are an excellent fortifier before facing the rigours of the supermarket. To help avoid the battles over crisps and sweets as you heave the trolley round, it is worth fuelling up before you leave. Such a policy can prevent children sucumbing to the lure of additive-loaded 'goodies' on the shelves. Avocados have a very high proportion of oil, almost a quarter of their weight, and it is mostly mono-unsaturated. This, together with their relatively high protein content and the fact that they contain only a fraction less vitamin C than blackcurrants, make them a very worthwhile food for children. Babies often like their bland flavour, making them a good early solid.

Melba toast usually goes down better than slices of ordinary toast. It is very simple to prepare and a good sized batch can easily be prepared in advance and frozen. It thaws under the grill in seconds. Unripe avocados never taste as good as smoothly ripe ones—and they don't mash well either. I tend to buy my avocados expecting to leave them in the fruit bowl to ripen for a few days before I can use them. You can speed up the process, though only slightly, by putting them in a brown paper bag and leaving them somewhere fairly warm. I have given a couple of suggestions for turning this snack into something a bit more substantial at the end of the recipe.

Leaving the crusts on the bread, toast it on both sides. While the toast is still hot, slice off the crusts and use the bread knife to slide between the two toasted sides and separate them. Cut each side into fingers or triangles. They should be left to cool in a single layer or they will steam each other up and become soggy. When they are cold, they can be bagged and frozen for future use or just left on one side until you are ready to use them.

Mash the avocado with the lemon juice (fresh is better than the sort with preservatives) until it is smooth. Heat the grill and toast the triangles, untoasted side up, for a few seconds. They toast very quickly, so keep your eye on them to avoid a smoke filled kitchen. Spread with avocado cream.

For a more filling spread, add any one of the following to one medium sized avocado and serve with a small salad and/or separate triangles of Melba toast:

- 2 oz (55g) plain boiled red lentils and a teaspoon of miso—good source of protein, calcium, iron and B vitamins (including B_{12}).

or

- 2 oz (55g) finely chopped dried figs (soak for 10 minutes in hot water first)—an excellent source of calcium, iron and B vitamins.

or

- 2 oz (55g) finely chopped dried apricots (soak for 10 minutes in hot water first)—very rich in protein, calcium, iron, and vitamins A and B_5.

Monster's Toenail Clippings

Another fried snack that is tasty hot or cold and travels well for packed lunches. 'Healthfood' lunches can be a source of embarrassment to children, and it is a fact that a high number of them end up in the school bin instead of the school child. The crisp- and sweet-eating brigade can down their lunch in a matter of minutes, while the health conscious lunch box can take quite a while to get through. This can lead to teasing, as the philistines dash out much earlier to the playground, so a powerful incentive for ditching the healthy lunch develops. A little consideration is called for when planning packed lunches. Two carrots, a sliver of cheese and a bean salad, an apple and an oat biscuit may seem ideal, but just think how long it will take to chew through it all. As a general rule, supply food that is quick and convenient to consume. An orange may be a useful source of vitamin C but it can be hell to peel while attempting to remain juice free. Above all, consult your child on a regular basis to check that all is well. If you don't ask, you can't expect to know what the problems are. Toenail Clippings will appeal to children's lurid imagination as well as their palate. They freeze well if you want to prepare a large batch.

4 oz (115g) chick pea flour
1 teaspoon (5ml) baking powder
4 oz (115g) bean sprouts
1 small red pepper
4 oz (115g) drained tinned sweetcorn kernels
1 tablespoon (15ml) shoyu
5–6 tablespoons (75–90ml) cold water

Mix the sieved chick pea flour with the baking powder. Wash and slice the pepper into long thin strips, about the same size as the bean sprouts. Add the shoyu and water to the flour and stir well, a few lumps won't matter. This mixing stage must be done immediately before frying because once the baking powder is wet, it will become active. If you don't use it quickly, it will fizz away and have expended its energy pointlessly, instead of lightening the batter. Add the pepper strips, bean sprouts and sweetcorn, and mix them into the batter, which should have a fairly thick consistency. Have ready some hot oil for deep frying (or shallow fry if you prefer). I find peanut oil is the best. Gently lower tablespoonfuls into the hot oil and fry the Clippings until brown and crisp. Drain them well and serve hot or cold with a sliced tomato and perhaps a spoonful or two of live yogurt or extra soy sauce for dipping. For more sophisticated palates, try adding a little fresh grated ginger, a touch of garlic and a hint of cumin to the batter.

Dragon's Eyeballs

Prepare the mashed potato 'eye sockets' in quantity when you are in the mood and stock up the freezer. They only take a minute or two to thaw in the microwave, or 20–30 minutes in a conventional oven. Again, the Eyeballs can be large or small to suit any appetite. There is no need to add salt to the potatoes. While it is true that bodies need salt (about 1 gram per day), this is easily obtained from the food we eat. Children (and adults) do not need extra salt, and it should not be added to their food, not even during hot sweaty weather. Approximately 20 per cent of children suffer from anaemia to some extent—a most unsatisfactory state of affairs. Ensure that your children are given plenty of iron rich foods like spinach, almonds, dates and cereals like Weetabix, muesli and brown rice as well as the other items mentioned in the previous recipes.

For 1 Eyeball
4–6 heaped tablespoons (60–90ml) potato mashed with ¼ teaspoon mixed spice
4 tablespoons (60ml) puréed spinach
1 tomato
1 small egg

Have ready a lightly greased oven tray. Make a small heap of potato on the tray and shape it into an oval. The base should be fairly thin with the sides built up to contain a generous quantity of spinach as well as the egg and tomato. I use my fingers to shape the potato but you could use a piping bag if you prefer. Use a fork to rough up the surface. If the potato is very dry and crumbly, add just a touch of milk to bind it. Fill the socket first with a layer of spinach which should be fairly dry. Either boil it rapidly to reduce the water or drain it in a sieve. Roughly chop the tomato and poke bits into the spinach. Your child may prefer the tomato to be skinned, in which case drop it into a bowl of freshly boiled water and leave it for a minute. Lift it out and you will find the skin peels away easily. The tomato represents the bloodshot veins of an overworked, fire-breathing green-eyed dragon. If the discerning child prefers his dragon bright-eyed or simply doesn't like tomato, you could omit it or exchange it for a little red pepper. Push the spinach and tomato well up the sides and leave a good dip for the raw egg to fit into with a clear border of green and red. Bake the Eyeball in a moderate oven, 350°F/180°C (gas mark 4), for just long enough to heat the Eye and firm the egg—about 10–15 minutes. If spinach is out of the question, try cottage cheese with a little puréed watercress and a tablespoon of yoghurt, or a purée of onions, peas, turnip or swede, with an ounce or two of ground almonds. If all else fails, baked beans are very nutritious!

Harlequin Muffins

A simple idea that can virtually become a meal in itself. There is hardly a set recipe for Harlequin Muffins as almost anything can be used to make them, provided you give a little thought to the final balance of textures and colours. Use either muffins or crumpets. Both freeze well. I often stock up with several packets and put them straight in the freezer when I get back from the supermarket. Wholemeal muffins are best, but you will doubtless be guided by what your child is prepared to eat. Harlequin Muffins are another option for the lunch box as they are good hot or cold and survive the rigours of the journey to school quite well. I have given ideas for savoury as well as sweet muffins.

Opposite Savoury Westmorland Loaf (page 20) and Simple Summer Instant Meal (page 18).

Basic Recipe for Savoury Harlequin Muffins

1 wholemeal muffin (or 2 crumpets)
1 tablespoon (15ml) tomato purée
pinch mixed herbs
½ small onion finely chopped
½ green or red pepper finely chopped
1 oz (30g) cheese

Toast the muffin on both sides, then split it. Or if you are using crumpets, toast the bottoms only. Spread the untoasted sides with tomato purée and sprinkle with mixed herbs. Cut the cheese into small dice and distribute between the two halves. Top with a generous sprinkling of onion and pepper. Put the muffins back under the grill until they are bubbling hot and the vegetables have softened slightly. Serve hot with a little salad, or cool and wrap for the lunch box.

I use any cheese I happen to have in, but it should be one that melts well. Harlequin Muffins need never be the same with imaginative use of whatever you happen to have at hand. Always start with a layer of tomato purée and follow with a layer of cheese. This will ensure a nice moist base. After that it's entirely up to you. Any of the following are candidates for interesting toppings. Use only three or four at a time, or even just one or two. Too many flavours at a time are rarely a good idea.

Parmesan
pine kernels
cottage cheese
Edam
sweetcorn kernels
hard boiled egg
smoked tofu
pineapple
olives
Brie
any kind of chutney or pickle
Cheddar
mushrooms
spinach
bean sprouts
beans
capers
Camembert
Mozzarella
sultanas
celery
artichoke hearts

Opposite Monster's Toenail Clippings (page 30) and Cheesy Tractor Wheels (page 27).

Basic Recipe for Sweet Harlequin Muffins

1 wholemeal muffin (or 2 crumpets)
1 tablespoon (15ml) runny honey
1 oz (30g) roughly chopped walnuts
1 teaspoon (5ml) cinnamon
1 tablespoon (15ml) raisins or sultanas

Toast the muffin on both sides, then split in two. Toast the crumpet bottoms only. Spread the untoasted sides with a very thin layer of honey. Sprinkle over with chopped walnuts and raisins. Drizzle over with the remaining honey and sprinkle with cinnamon. Return to the grill until hot and bubbly.

There are lots of items that you can use to make sweet Harlequin Muffins. Always start and finish with a layer of honey, low sugar jam, maple syrup or golden syrup, but bear in mind that they should be used as sparingly as possible. It is best to choose two or three items for a topping—too many and the flavours become a messy hodge podge—and aim for a mixture of crisp and soft, such as banana and pecans, or chocolate and sunflower seeds.

chopped prunes
chopped apricots
grated carob
pear
apple
chopped almonds
pecans
pineapple
crunchy muesli
chopped dates
grated chocolate
peach
banana
plum
hazelnuts
pine kernels
sunflower seeds
cashew nuts

You can also use flavourings such as ginger, mixed spice and finely grated lemon peel.

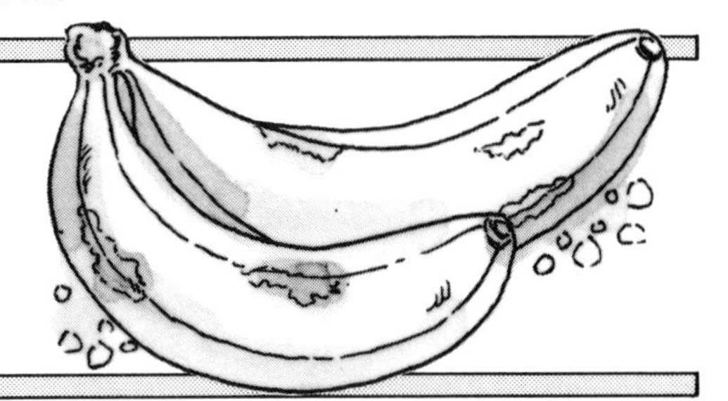

Fruit Baskets

Vegetarian children often miss out on jellies, the conventional sort being set with the residues from boiled animal bones and tissues. Agar is a sea vegetable gelling agent, and makes a very good alternative to animal based gelatine. The set it gives is rather firmer than animal jelly, but nevertheless it is pretty good. These jelly baskets make a good party dish, particularly if you spend time cutting the oranges apart with a zig-zag movement to give a spiked finish. Rich in vitamin C, with added calcium, minerals and vitamin A from the banana, this is a very nutritious sweet. The jelly could be packed in small tubs for inclusion in the lunch box if it proves to be a favourite.

For 4 baskets
2 large oranges
1 small banana
½ small lemon
6 - 7 oz (170 - 200 g) frozen concentrated orange juice
3 tablespoons (45 ml) agar flakes or 2 teaspoons (10 ml) powdered agar

Slice the orange in two and squeeze out as much juice as possible, but keep the skin intact. Place the juice in a measuring jug. Scoop out the flesh and discard it, leaving clean, empty shells. Reserve the shells to serve the jelly in. Slice the banana into small chunks and dip them in lemon juice. Drain the banana chunks, put on one side. Make up the fresh and concentrated orange juice to 1 pint (570 ml) with water. Taste the juice for sweetness—you may feel a teaspoon or two (5-10ml) of honey is needed, but it will depend very much on your taste buds.

If you are using powdered agar, place it in a small saucepan and add one or two tablespoons (15–30ml) of the measured fruit juice. Mix it to a smooth cream, with no lumps, before adding the rest of the juice to the pan. If you are using agar flakes, put all the fruit juice in the pan and sprinkle the flakes on top. Bring the juice to the boil, stirring all the time. Simmer until the agar has disappeared and the liquid looks almost clear. The flakes will take up to 2–3 minutes, the powder will dissolve in a few seconds. Allow the hot jelly to cool a little before adding the banana chunks. Pour into a shallow dish and allow at least an hour in a cool place for it to set. Cut the sheet of jelly into bite size chunks and pile them into the hollowed-out orange shells just before serving.

Space Pebbles

More commonly known as nuts roasted in shoyu or tamari, these tasty treats are a low fat, high protein snack—the perfect answer when breakfast was ignored and lunch was half a banana. They also make a healthy change from low-fibre, high-fat crisps. Your own version of dry roasted nuts without the additives, and a snack which dentists prefer to chewy, tooth-rotting sweets. If you keep the health aspect to yourself, I'm sure Space Pebbles will become an enduring favourite. Any nut can be roasted in this way. Cashews are my favourite, but try peanuts, almonds or even cooked chick peas (rich in B vitamins) for a change. They fit handily into a packed school lunch and also go down very well with a glass of wine when the hard pressed parent can afford to relax! In general, it is never wise to give children food to eat as they watch television. Little notice is taken of the food, it just goes down—hardly a healthy way to eat. On the other hand, if that is one of the ways that you get nourishment into your child, you could do a lot worse than a dish of Space Pebbles.

8 oz (225g) broken cashews
6 tablespoons (90ml) shoyu or tamari

Shoyu is another name for natural soy sauce. Tamari is soy sauce that has been prepared without wheat grains and is therefore gluten-free, unlike shoyu. Despite this difference, I find the flavours virtually identical. Some sauces are merely a concoction of caramel and chemical flavourings. 'Naturally brewed' are the words to look for on the label. To save washing up, I usually roast the nuts on a piece of tin foil. If this seems too profligate, put the nuts directly into a shallow tray. The tray should be able to accommodate the nuts in one layer. Pour over the shoyu or tamari, and ensure all the nuts are well coated. Bake in a moderate oven, 350°F/180°C (gas mark 4), for 15 minutes. Delicious!

Nuts and Bolts

Carob coated clusters of cashew nuts and apricots or sunflower seeds and raisins. A treat for the sweet tooth, and one of those items that your children can prepare for themselves. There is no need for any added sweeteners as the dried fruit and carob provide all that is required. Carob isn't so much a substitute for chocolate as a nutritious food in its own right. It is naturally sweet, unlike chocolate, and therefore does not need to be made palatable with vast quantities of sugar. The low sugar content together with the absence of the stimulant theo bromine, which is present in chocolate, make it an altogether healthier alternative. Carob also contains significant quantities of B vitamins as well as minerals, making these lumpy little sweets an excellent addition to the lunch box. They go down well at afternoon play gatherings and can provide a happy morning's activity as your child gets to grips with food preparation. A little supervision is required while the carob bar is melted, but other than that a glorious time can be had weighing, mixing and shaping. Nuts and Bolts are also another handy energy booster and distracter from unacceptable sweets in the supermarket. If you don't like the idea of sticky carob covered fingers while out shopping, try the Peanut and Wheatgerm goodies that follow this recipe.

4 oz (115g) bar milk or plain carob
4 oz (115g) broken cashew nut pieces
4 oz (115g) chopped apricots

or

4 oz (115g) bar milk or plain carob
4 oz (115g) sunflower seed
4 oz (15g) raisins or sultanas

Break the carob bar into pieces (or use carob drops) and melt in a large bowl over simmering water. I find one of the easiest ways is to stand the bowl on a toasting or cooling rack which is sitting squarely on top of a good sized pan of gently simmering water. This, of course, must be organized by an adult.

When the carob is melted, stand the bowl on a folded tea towel for stability and tip in the rest of the ingredients and mix together. Pile little clusters of the mixture into petit four cases and allow to harden.

Peanut and Wheatgerm Goodies

Another recipe that is excellent both for children to cook themselves and as a supermarket nibble. Based on peanut butter and dried skimmed milk powder, these sweets are high in protein, another useful option when not much else is being eaten—a perfect example of quality not quantity. But don't forget that they are really quite high in calories and just because they contain 'healthy' ingredients, that is no reason for over-indulgence! The mixture makes about 20 sweets.

2 tablespoons (30ml) crunchy or smooth peanut butter
2 tablespoons (30ml) thick honey
2 oz (55g) chopped figs or raisins or dates or apricots
1 oz (30g) dried milk powder
1 oz (30g) wheatgerm
1 oz (30g) sunflower seeds
A little coconut or sesame seeds or carob or chopped nuts or wheatgerm for rolling

Blend all the ingredients together. It's a gloriously sticky mess which requires lots of rubbing to mix everything evenly. Form into marble-sized balls. The mixture will seem fairly dry and crumbly, but if you dampen the palms of your hands as you roll the balls you will find they form quite easily. Roll the balls in the coating of your choice.

You can ring the changes by making your own nut butter by grinding 2 oz (55g) cashews or almonds with a teaspoon of oil instead of using peanut butter, and swapping the wheatgerm for sesame seeds. The variations, as with so many vegetarian recipes, are endless. I'd be pleased to hear about your own favourite flexible recipe!

Teddy Bear's Paw Prints

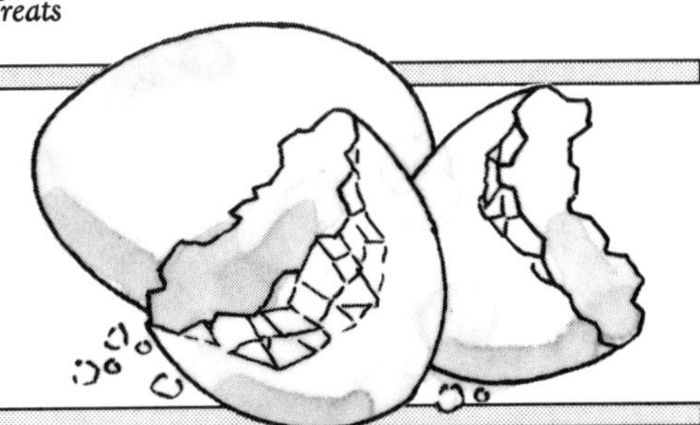

These delightful pancakes cum fritters are made with corn meal, a gluten free 'flour' which supplies vitamin A, B vitamins, calcium and magnesium as well as protein and fibre. Use the coarse variety to give an interesting grainy texture to the Paw Prints. I use Polenta, the one described as cooking in 5 minutes. I find very finely ground corn or maize meal a bit too fine for this recipe. Polenta is used to make a traditional Italian cheese pudding, apparently once a favourite of Napoleon I. Teddy Bear's Paws are every bit as simple, but rather quicker to prepare, than traditional Polenta pudding and an excellent introduction to a very useful ingredient. Serve them sweet or savoury as your child prefers. Leftover untopped Paws freeze well.

4 oz (115g) 5-minute Polenta
1 egg
6-7 tablespoons (90-105ml) cold water
1 or 2 tablespoons (15-30ml) oil for frying

Mix the corn meal, egg and water together to give a soft dropping consistency like a good cake mix, rather than a runny batter. Heat the oil in a large frying pan—use peanut oil or olive for preference—and drop tablespoons of the mixture into the pan. Press the Paws down a little with the back of a spoon or spatula. Cook the first side for 2 or 3 minutes then flip it over and cook the other side.

Serve the Paws at once with any of the listed toppings, or sample them with the thinnest drizzle of honey and a generous dusting of cinnammon. For a more adult approach, try really small Paws dusted with cayenne, and, needless to say, a glass of wine—they'll revive any flagging parent.

Topping ideas:

honey and chopped pear
mashed banana and orange juice
fruit and thick yogurt
low sugar jam and flaked almonds
stewed apple and sultanas
cottage cheese
mashed avacado
spinach and thick yogurt
miso or Marmite
peanut butter and tomato

3.

A Batch of Baking

Choosing Sugar for Baking

I almost always choose white granulated sugar for baking. If I want fine caster, I simply run ordinary granulated through my food processor for a few minutes to make it really fine. What, you may ask, is a healthy vegetarian doing proposing white sugar instead of wholesome brown? In a nutshell, there is no such thing as 'good' sugar, so I use white because it is cheap.

Molasses is the most unrefined of the sugars, yet in contains only 5 per cent minerals. The other 95 per cent is sugar and water, which have no nutritional value at all. Treacle, honey, syrup and brown sugar all contain even less by way of beneficial nutrients, and more unhealthy sugar, until at the bottom of the scale we have pure, white 100 per cent sugar. Now you may feel that the tiny quantity of minerals present in molasses, which the body can benefit from, makes it worth using. I don't. I'd rather get my minerals from healthier foods. In the final analysis, all sugars are unhealthy, there is no way round it. I use white sugar to bake with because its whiteness is the perfect, built-in reminder, that the substance I am using really is 'pure, white and deadly'. If I used one of the brown sugars, given that sweet things are so irresistible, I might well be tempted to let myself eat more because I could pretend Brown=Healthy. It doesn't, but we all know how things are when temptation is looking sweetly up from the plate!

Concentrated fruit juice? Well, fructose (fruit sugar) is easier to metabolize and suitable for diabetics. Fructose is also extremely sweet so, at least in theory less is required. But fructose often contains cheaper sugar syrups to bulk out the fruit sugar. And the fact remains that even if the product is 100 per cent fructose, it is still a refined sugar, and all refined sugars are too easy to over-consume. The only way to cope with them is to eat less.

The NACNE report recommends that we all cut sugar consumption by at least 50 per cent. My solution is to use white sugar, or the unbleached variety which is now available, for those who are concerned about chemicals. At least I keep a fairly clear idea of what I'm using and eating, it's cheap, gives good light results in cakes and puddings, and ensures meringues, sorbets etc. look attractively pale. If you prefer to stick to the so-called 'healthy sugars' so be it. But in my opinion, the only times expensive unrefined brown sugars are worthwhile are in gingerbread parkin, rich fruit cake and the like, for their undeniably delicious flavours. The answer is to cut down on sweet foods altogether. They have to become rare and special treats: sad, but true.

Choosing Fats for Baking

More heresy, I'm afraid. I use butter for baking and olive, peanut (groundnut) and sesame oils (cold pressed—what else?) for all other purposes. NACNE recommend that fats should provide no more than 30 per cent of our total energy intake and saturated fats should be no more than 10 per cent. I feel that in the average vegetarian diet, fats represent a smaller part than for the average meat eater, and therefore the vegetarian does not need to be quite so careful. Nevertheless, I hear you say, butter?

First it should be said that most baking uses a fair amount of fat and sugar. Fats and sugars are not healthy items when consumed in quantity and so it follows that baked goods are generally not too healthy either. One of the reasons I bake with butter is that I don't do it too often, so the butter isn't too bad! The other elements in my choice of butter are more difficult to explain.

Margarines are highly processed foods, in which the manufacturer uses all the technological aids available. I don't trust manufacturers to use ingredients that won't harm my health, so, on the whole, I don't trust margarines. They are usually plastic substances, carefully engineered, bursting with preservatives, colourings, emulsifiers and flavourings, designed to appear acceptable regardless of their contents. Read a label and you'll see what I mean!

Margarine and butter contain the same amount of fat. The law says they must. If a spread is 'low fat' or 'half the fat' then of course what the packet states is true. What it may omit to mention is that the fat content is low because the water content is high—very cost effective from the manufacturer's point of view. How clever to get us paying for water! That is why low fat products spit and splutter if you try to fry with them, and usually give dismal results in cakes and baking generally.

Finally, saturated versus poly-unsaturated. Many margarines are made with poly-unsaturated oils. Oil is runny and margarine isn't. In most margarines, manufacturers get round this problem by using a process called hydrogenation. This means the oil is treated with hydrogen gas, which induces it to become solid rather than liquid. Hydrogenation also turn poly-unsaturates into saturates, so the product is no longer what you might have thought it to be. Again, you must read the label. It isn't an accident that ingredients are listed in small print in my opinion, so don't forget to take you glasses to the supermarket! Even if you feel that poly-unsaturate margarine is healthy (and I don't, but that's another story) it isn't just a matter of picking up the first vegetable oil margarine your hand falls on.

In the same way as white sugar, so it is with butter: you know what the score is. A good quality, unsalted butter, free from nasty additives, gets my vote every time. It gives light results, tastes delicious, and there isn't a shadow of a doubt that I know it must be kept to a minimum. I except concentrated butter from my recommendation. It is super-concentrated, saturated fat, and therefore to be avoided. Furthermore, buying it helps reduce Food Mountains to manageable proportions, which in turn enables the EEC to continue ducking this disgraceful issue.

For the vegan, I would recommend *Tomor* or *Vitaquell* instead of butter. *Tomor* is a completely animal-free product but it is saturated fat, so, like butter, should be used sparingly. The only other margarine that I feel to be acceptable is *Vitaquell*. It is dairy-free, salt-free, unhydrogenated and high in poly-unsaturates—it even contains a high level of vitamin E.

Oils are discussed in the Stocking Up section on page 82.

Choosing Flour for Baking

The question of which flour to choose for baking is one that has caused a remarkable amount of confusion. Flour starts life as grains of wheat. A wheat grain has a fibrous outer layer, which when milled becomes bran, a starchy middle called the endosperm and a small, oily heart, knows as the germ, the wheatgerm. The starchy endosperm makes up 85 per cent of the grain, the fibrous outer coat 12 per cent and the germ 3 per cent. This then is what the miller uses to make the multiplicity of flours that are now available. Broadly speaking there are three types of wheat flour.

Wholemeal or wholewheat flour which is made from the whole grain. It is called '100 per cent extraction' because the flour contains 100 per cent of the grain. There has been much misunderstanding about the term 'wheatmeal'. 'Wheatmeal' flour did not contain 100 per cent of the grain, though many people were confused into thinking it did. This misleading term was dropped from use in 1986 but somehow the confusion still lingers. The prefix 'whole' whether followed by 'meal' or 'wheat' now means the flour is 100 per cent of the grain. Because wholemeal flour contains nutritionally valuable wheatgerm, it does not keep as well as the other flours. The oil in the wheatgerm becomes rancid after about 2 months, which is why it is worth buying a little flour often, rather than stocking up. Many people prefer their flour 'stone-ground'. The grains are ground between slowly rotating mill stones, rather than the industrial millers, 20 or 30 high speed rollers, sifters and purifiers. The stones grind the wheat gently, without raising the temperature to the high levels in the industial milling process. In this way the beneficial oils in the germ remain intact.

Brown flours include a multitude of types. Brown flour is lacking only a small proportion of the bran of 100 per cent wholemeal flours—usually 15 per cent. Therefore 85 per cent of the grain remains and that is why brown flour is usually described as '85 per cent extraction', though it can vary between 80 per cent and 90 per cent. Wheatgerm flour is enriched with processed wheatgerm, Granary and Malted wheat flours are enriched with crushed and malted grains and Bran flour with added bran fibre. All these fall into the category of brown flour. Stoneground brown flours are readily available, usually at 81 per cent or 85 per cent extractions. Stoneground brown flour usually contains wheatgerm, unlike industrially milled brown flours, from which it is removed.

White flour has had around 25 per cent to 30 per cent of the whole grain removed and is between 72 per cent and 74 per cent extraction. White flour is mostly starchy endosperm, all the bran and wheatgerm have been removed. The bran and germ will be sold for animal feeds, pet foods and health food products. White flour is fortified with B vitamins, thiamin, nicotinic acid and iron (sadly, this is ferric rather than ferrous iron and the body cannot absorb it properly) to make up, at least in part, for what is lost in the milling process. Both brown and white flours are higher in calcium than wholemeal flour because they contain added chalk.

As for what to bake with? Firstly I prefer to buy plain flours, no matter if it's wholemeal, brown or white. I can then add a raising agent of my own choice, if and when I want it. My own preference is for 80 per cent to 85 per cent extraction, stoneground, brown flour. If I can't get brown flour, then I opt for 100 per cent wholemeal and generally sieve a little of the bran out myself. The bran and wheatgerm content of flours affect the 'rise' and give that close texture familiar in wholemeal and brown flours. Such flours are also often 'strong' flours, meaning they have a high gluten content, ideal for breadmaking, but creating hard pastry and cakes. English and European winter wheats make 'soft' flour with a low gluten content, less satisfactory for bread, but much better for cakes and pastry. The addition of a little lemon juice to strong wholemeal or brown flour cake and pastry mixes helps make soft cakes and crumbly pastry. Use unbleached white flour for preference and bear in mind that 'soft' or 'strong' applies equally to all the flours, so it is worth reading labels—'strong' bread flour makes poor pastry; 'soft' cake flour makes disappointing bread. If you are new to wholemeal flour, try mixing it 50/50 with your usual flour or even one quarter wholemeal or brown and three-quarters of your usual. Get used to the different taste and texture gradually.

Wholemeal Pastry that Really Works

The secret of success is not odd quantities of sugar or baking powder but classic proportions of fat and flour and, the real secret, a few drops of lemon juice. Soft, crumbly, wholemeal pastry really is possible!

Pastry sufficient for one 8 inch (20cm) flan ring:
6 oz (170g) plain wholemeal or brown flour
3 oz (85g) butter
juice of ½ lemon
3-4 tablespoons (45-60ml) cold water

Don't use self-raising flour to make pastry, it tends to make it tough. I never bother to sieve the flour, its seems to me a waste of always restricted time! Rub the fat into the flour until it looks like fine breadcrumbs. Make the lemon juice up to ¼ pint (150ml) with cold water. Wholemeal flour varies in its capacity to absorb water, so it is impossible to give more than a guide to how much you will need. Add enough lemon/water to achieve a moist dough. The ball should leave the sides of the mixing bowl clean when rolled around. Wholemeal pastry should be made just a little wetter than white flour pastry.

Rest the ball of dough, wrapped in cling film or greaseproof paper, for at least 15 minutes in the fridge. This helps the acid in the lemon juice do its work and allows the dough to absorb the wetness. Take the pastry from the fridge, roll out and use as you would normally.

Pastry should always be cooked in a hot oven, and preferably on or in metal—porcelain may look prettier but it makes pastry bases soggy! If you are baking a pastry case which is to be filled later, line the unbaked pastry with tin foil, bake in a hot oven 425°F/220°C (gas mark 7) for 15 minutes, remove the foil and bake for a further 5 minutes to dry it off.

Tomor can be substituted for butter to make vegan pastry.

Arrowroot and Bay Leaf Custard Tart with Fresh Peaches

A lovely old-fashioned way of flavouring this tart for tea-time or pudding. Set it in one large or several individual pastry cases. The fruit for the topping can be varied depending on the season.

1 × 8 inch (20cm) baked flan case (page 44)
1 pint (570ml) milk
2 tablespoons (30ml) sugar
6 bay leaves
2 tablespoons (30ml) arrowroot
2 egg yolks
2 fresh peaches
1 tablespoon (15ml) apricot jam

Reserve two or three tablespoons (30–45ml) of milk. Bring the rest to the boil. Add the sugar and bay leaves and remove immediately from the heat. Leave to infuse for at least 20 minutes. Mix the arrowroot with the reserved milk. Remove the bay leaves from the milk in the pan and bring it back to the boil. Pour the arrowroot onto the boiling milk, whisking all the while. Boil the mixture for ½ minute to cook the arrowroot. Remove the pan from the heat and allow to cool slightly, then whisk in the egg yolks. Pour the hot, aromatic custard into the ready baked flan case, smoothing the surface. Allow to cool completely. Wash and finely slice the peaches and lay them, overlapping, around the edge of the tart. To give an attractive glaze, melt the apricot jam and brush it over the fruit slices. Lightly stewed dried apple slices, kiwi fruits or fresh orange segments can be substituted for the peaches.

Gingered Rhubarb with Oatmeal Crumble

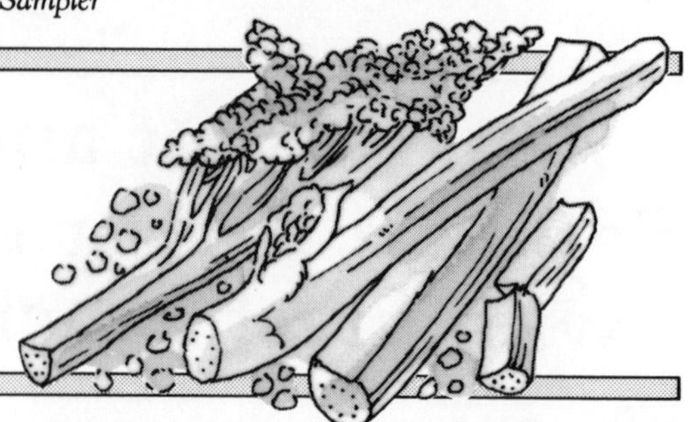

Present it in a dainty dish with a jug of single cream for a special occasion or, on a more everyday level, with a jug of skimmed milk or a generous splot of yogurt or sweetened silken tofu. It really is quite delicious.

Crumble topping:
4 oz (115g) wholemeal flour
3 oz (85g) jumbo oats
2 oz (55g) sugar
1 oz (30g) wheatgerm

Gingered rhubarb:
1½ lb (680g) rhubarb
4 tablespoons (60ml) green ginger wine

Rub together all the ingredients for the crumble topping. Wash the fruit and slice it into 2 inch (5cm) pieces. Pile the fruit into a deep-ish dish about 8 inches (20 cm) in diameter. Pour over the ginger wine. If the rhubarb is particularly sour, add a little sugar or honey, but the wine will be sweetening enough for most rhubarb. Top with the crumble mixture, patting it well down—but don't squash it flat!

Bake for 30–40 minutes in a medium oven 375°F/190°C (gas mark 5). Serve hot, warm or cold. If the occasion is special and calories aren't too important, try serving it with the following: Whisk one or two egg whites till stiff. Whisk a carton of double cream till stiff and fold it into the beaten egg whites with one or two tablespoons (15–30ml) of green ginger wine. You could use crème fraîche for a slightly lower calorie count than double cream (it won't need whipping).

Use *Tomor* instead of butter to make vegan rhubarb crumble.

Mrs Monroe's Spice Bake

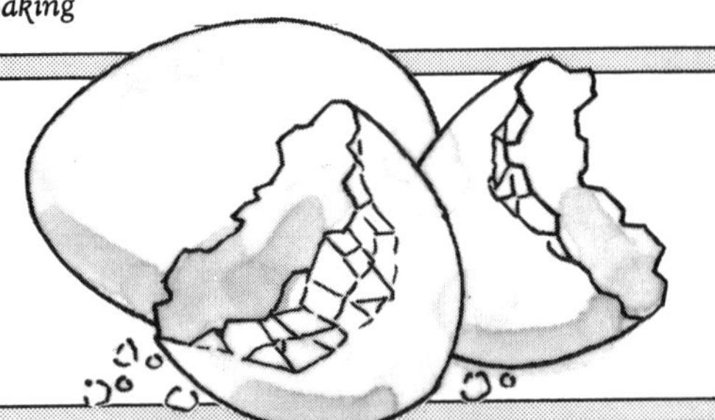

The ingredients for the 'bread' element are only a guide, almost any proportion of bread, cake or buns will do—very useful for coping with leftovers in the bottom of the cake tin, the bread bin and even the biscuit tin!

4 oz (115g) wholemeal bread
4 oz (115g) dry cake leftovers—any kind
4 oz (115g) stale teacake or fruit bun
4 tablespoons (60ml) low-sugar jam—any kind
2 eggs
1 pint (570ml) milk
2 teaspoons (10ml) mixed spice
2 tablespoons (30ml) sugar

Cut the bread, cakes and buns into cubes about 1 inch (2.5cm) square. Whisk the egg yolks (reserve the whites), milk, mixed spice and half the low-sugar jam together and pour over the bread mixture, mixing it all well together. Allow to stand for 30 minutes, then tip into a lightly greased dish and bake in a cool oven 275°F/140°C (gas mark 2) for 1–1½ hours.

Whisk the egg whites till stiff and fold in the sugar. Spread the top of the pudding with the remaining low-sugar jam, then cover with meringue and return to the cool oven for a further hour. If you prefer soft meringue, flash in a hot oven for just 5 minutes.

This dish is excellent hot or cold with dried fruit compôte or custard—or both! Ring the changes by adding a chopped apple, a few nuts or a handful of mixed dried fruit to the basic mixture.

Vegans could omit the eggs and use bean milk instead of cow's milk, though, of course, there will be no meringue topping. Try it with a cream made by whizzing a carton of silken tofu with a tablespoon of maple syrup.

Almond and Apricot Cake

The quickest and most simple cake there could ever be. It tastes absolutely delicious and it doesn't even need a mixing bowl!

8 oz (225g) butter
5 oz (140g) sugar
10 oz (285g) plain wholemeal flour
2 large eggs
2 teaspoons (10ml) baking powder
4 oz (115g) finely chopped dried apricots*
2 oz (55g) roughly chopped almonds

Have ready a greased 8 inch (20cm) cake tin. Melt the butter and sugar together in a good sized pan. Tip in the flour, baking powder, eggs, apricots and almonds (I never bother to blanch them) and beat well. Work quickly—once the baking powder is wet it starts to work so the cake should go into the oven as quickly as possible. Tip the mixture into the greased tin and smooth the top. Bake at 350°F/180°C (gas mark 4) for 30–40 minutes.

If you wish, the cake can be decorated with a ring of almonds and/or apricots before it goes into the oven. If they show signs of overcooking, cover them with a sheet of tin foil or greaseproof paper. Alternatively, decorate the top with dried fruits and nuts after baking, using melted apricot jam as both glue and glaze. This cake freezes well.

*Most apricots are treated with sulphur and mineral oil, neither of which is good for health. Choose apricots that have not undergone this process—you can really taste the difference! If the apricots are very hard and dry, soak them in hot water for 10 minutes before drying them well and chopping. Take a good tablespoon (15ml) of flour from the given quantity and rub it into the apricots to help stop the pieces sticking together.

Marmalade and Walnut Cake

This recipe is based on the same principles as the previous cake and is every bit as simple and delicious.

8 oz (225g) butter
5 oz (140g) sugar
10 oz (285g) plain wholemeal flour
2 small eggs
2 teaspoons (10ml) baking powder
2 teaspoons (10ml) mixed spice
3½ oz (100g) chopped walnuts
2 tablespoons (30ml) marmalade

Have ready a greased 8 inch (20cm) cake tin. Melt the butter and sugar together. Tip in the flour, eggs, baking powder, mixed spice, chopped walnuts and one tablespoon (15ml) of marmalade. Beat well together and tip into the greased cake tin, smoothing the top. Bake at 350°F/180°C (gas mark 4) for 30–40 minutes. Melt the remaining marmalade and brush it over the top of the cake while it is still hot.

For freezing, cut into individual slices for economical use, it also helps the sinning slimmer to consume one slice instead of . . . well . . . we all know the temptations of large cakes!

Sultana Cake with Molasses

This is a wonderfully soft, moist, dark cake. Its lightness is proof that wholemeal baking doesn't have to be heavy and lumpen.

1 lb (455g) plain wholemeal flour
2 teaspoons (10ml) cinnamon
1 teaspoon (5ml) mixed spice
6 oz (170g) butter
4 oz (115g) sugar
2 teaspoons (10ml) bicarbonate of soda
8 oz (225g) sultanas
12 fl oz (340ml) milk
2 rounded tablespoons (30-40ml) molasses

Rub all the dry ingredients into the butter until the mixture looks like fine bread crumbs. Stir in the sultanas. Whisk the molasses and milk together. Pour it onto the rubbed in mixture and beat well to make a smooth, soft dropping consistency mixture. Turn it into a 9 or 10 inch (23–25cm) lightly greased tin and bake at 350°F/180°C (gas mark 4) for 1–1½ hours.

Use bean milk and *Tomor* for a vegan cake.

Crumble Crisps

Oaty biscuits that are quick to cook and unusually flavoured. Bake them at the same time as one of the cakes given on the previous pages and you'll have a splendid stock of home bakes for remarkably little effort.

4 oz (115g) butter
2 oz (55g) golden syrup
2 oz (5g) treacle
8 oz (225g) oats
8 oz (225g) wholemeal flour
1 tablespoon (15ml) ground ginger
1 tablespoon (15ml) whole aniseeds

Melt the butter, syrup and treacle together in a good sized pan. Remove from the heat and tip in the rest of the ingredients. The mixture quickly becomes fairly dry as the ingredients are worked together, so it is important to ensure that they are well mixed. Pour the mixture into a lightly greased Swiss roll tin, patting it well down, but not crushing it to death! Bake for 20–25 minutes at 375°F/190°C (gas mark 5). Cut into fingers while it is still hot—it becomes brittle as it cools.

Vegans should substitute *Tomor* for butter.

Sour Cream Scones

Sour cream enhances the raising power of the bicarbonate of soda and cream of tartar, giving a wonderfully light effect to what can all too often be very lumpen wholemeal scones.

2 oz (55g) butter
8 oz (225g) wholemeal flour
1 oz (30g) sugar
1 teaspoon (5ml) cream of tartar
1 teaspoon (5ml) bicarbonate of soda
2 oz (55g) sultanas
3 rounded tablespoons (60ml) sour cream
5-6 tablespoons (75-90ml) cold water

Rub the butter into the flour, sugar, cream of tartar and bicarbonate of soda. Mix in the sultanas. Put the sour cream into a jug and add 5 tablespoons of cold water stirring well to amalgamate it. Add the liquid to the scone mix. Wholemeal flour varies in its absorption powers and it may be necessary to add an extra tablespoon (15ml) of water to get a moist, but firm dough.

Roll the dough to about 1 inch (2.5cm) and cut into rounds. Brush the tops with milk or water and sprinkle with a little extra flour. Bake for 15 minutes at 400°F/200°C (gas mark 6).

For vegan scones, omit the sour cream and use water and *Tomor* instead of butter.

Date Castles

The dates in this recipe are used as a substitute for less healthy forms of sugar. Why not try some of your own recipes using creamed dates instead of brown or white sugar? This mixture makes 8 small or 6 large castles depending on your moulds. Eat them hot with custard for pudding or rolled in jam and coconut for a tea time treat.

4 oz (115g) stoned dates
¼ pint (140ml) water
2 oz (55g) butter
8 oz (225g) wholemeal flour
2 teaspoons (10ml) baking powder
1 egg
3 tablespoons (45ml) milk
1 teaspoon (5ml) vanilla essence

Oil or butter 6 or 8 dariole moulds. Put the dates into a small saucepan with the water, bring to the boil and simmer for 3–4 minutes. Cool them a little then add the egg, milk and vanilla essence and beat until smooth. Rub the butter into the flour and baking powder until you have a fine breadcrumb mixture.

Pour the dates onto the flour and beat the two together—a soft dropping consistency is what is required, so, depending on the flour, you may need an extra tablespoon (15ml) of milk. Spoon the mixture into the dariole moulds, filling them three-quarters full. Bake at 375°F/190°C (gas mark 5) for 25–30 minutes. Baked in a 1 lb (455g) loaf tin for 40 minutes, this mixture also makes a very acceptable tea loaf.

Spiced Cherry Jelly

I love cherries and this is a favourite recipe. Use it as a low-sugar spread and try it as an addition to just about any sweet. On warm, sour cream scones with clotted cream, it's a stunner. Healthy eating?.... tomorrow!

1 lb (455 g) frozen cherries
2 sticks cinnamon
1 small orange
8 cloves
2½ tablespoons (40 ml) agar flakes (or 2 round teaspoons (12 ml) agar powder)

Put the cherries (which I like to use whole, but you may prefer to chop them up) into a saucepan with ½ pint (285ml) water. Add the cinnamon sticks. Wash the orange and cut it into quarters, sticking two cloves into the peel on each quarter. Make a couple of cuts in the flesh to help the juices flow and add them to the pan. Bring to the boil and simmer for 10 minutes. Remove the cinnamon sticks and orange quarters.

Sprinkle the agar flakes onto the cherries and boil for 2 or 3 minutes to melt the agar. If you use agar powder, mix it to a paste with a little cold water before adding it to the cherries otherwise it is likely to get lumpy. Pour the slightly cooled jelly into jars and store in the fridge.

Don't forget the lack of sugar will mean the spread won't keep like ordinary jam. If you add an extra ½ tablespoon (7.5ml) of agar flakes or ¼ teaspoon (2ml) of powder the jelly will be firm enough to set and turn out. With the addition of extra sugar, the cherry spread makes a splendid filling for a ready baked pastry case.

Apricot and Almond Spread

This recipe makes three 1 lb (455g) jars of very low-sugar jam. Use it as a filling for sandwich cakes, on muffins or toast, or with a carton of thick yogurt for a quick protein- and iron-rich pudding.

8 oz (225g) unsulphured apricots
2 pints (1.1 litres) water
1 oz (30g) whole almonds
2 tablespoons (30ml) arrowroot
1 tablespoon (15ml) honey

Put the unsoaked apricots in a pan with the water and slivered almonds. Bring to the boil and simmer for 30–45 minutes until the apricots are completely soft and largely disintegrated. Mix the arrowroot to a cream with three tablespoons of cold water. Pour the arrowroot onto the simmering apricots and cook for a minute. Remove from the heat and cool a little. Sweeten the spread with honey, then pour it into clean jars and store in the fridge.

4.

Entertaining with Style

Entertaining does not have to mean hours spent in the kitchen or coping with incredibly complicated techniques suited only to a master chef. We all live in a busy world and entertaining must be geared to practicalities. I have set out three menus which are fit to entertain the most discerning guests, each quite different in its own way. The first is long and grand. It requires a reasonable amount of time and trouble for such a sumptuous banquet, but it is, nevertheless, within the capabilities of any cook. The second menu adopts a much simpler approach, less courses and less time in the kitchen. The third menu is for those occasions when you are compelled to entertain, despite lack of time and/or enthusiasm: or for a 'spur of the moment, decided at lunch time, cook it tonight' meal. It is quick, not shy to use convenience foods and yet has all the style of a superb meal.

There is something remarkably liberating about vegetarian entertaining. The food lends itself to a variety of small courses than can be endless in their variations. It seems to me so much more absorbing than building around the omnipresent piece of meat. I know, in the past, vegetarian food has been described as lumpen—not least by myself!—and deservedly so. The dishes in these menus are light, delicious and nutritious, and none of them are particularly complicated. I am not an advocate of dressing everyday foods like brown rice and beans in festival wreaths of parsley and calling them gourmet. A meat eater wouldn't present you with shepherd's pie and tell you it was an epicurean treat, so why should a vegetarian?

Entertain with flair and style, and show the poor old limited meat eater that there really is a world of delicious food that doesn't depend on churning out endless lumps of meat or, for that matter, insipid, high fibre grains.

The recipes in this section are for six. Many of them are easily adapted to vegan preferences by swapping butter for oil, cow's milk for bean milk and cream products for silken tofu.

An Entertainment in the Grand Style

Peppered Cob Nuts

Spiced nuts to nibble with a pre-prandial drink

Green Almond Soup

A smooth and creamy soup to start the meal

Mushroom Parcels served with Garlic Cream and Mangetout

A rich ragoût of mushrooms in crisp filo cases served with a puddle of smooth sauce and mangetout

Water Melon Sorbet

A delicate ice to refresh the palate between courses

Lord Liu An's Delight

Marinaded tofu pouches filled with parsley and pine kernels served with wild rice and cherry tomatoes

Persimmon Pies with Honey Cream

Individual fruit tarts spiced with cinnamon and Kirsch garnished with redcurrants

Nuggets of Golden Honeycomb and Coffee

Entertaining in Simpler Vein

Charentais Melon Perfumed with Ginger Wine

Fragrant individual melons with ginger wine

Roulade of Calabrese with Classic Orange Sauce

A rich roulade of pecans, pistachios and calabrese together with Potatoes Dauphinoise and artichoke bottoms filled with herbed carrots

Paskha Cassata

A Sicilian cassata or a Russian Paskha?
A wonderful combination of glacé fruits, chocolate and Marsala

Cheese Board

English cheeses served with pears and apples

Old Fashioned Peppermint Creams and Coffee

A Gourmet Meal in a Hurry

Asparagus and Orange Soup
A classic combination of flavours for a delicious start to the meal

Cucumber Terrine
A dainty round of cucumber and smoked tofu flavoured with dill

Leek and Pear Strudel with Cider Sauce
A crisp strudel of leeks, buckwheat and pears served with herbed potatoes, carrots and courgettes

Rose Water Mousse with Brandy Snaps
A smooth, sweet, rice cream topped with pomegranate seeds complemented with crisp biscuits

Cheese Board
French cheeses with a basket of dried fruits and nuts

Chocolates and Coffee

An Entertainment in the Grand Style

Despite that fact that this is a grand and sumptuous affair, with a little planning, the dishes are well within the competence of any cook. Begin cooking at least the day before the meal. Some of the dishes can be prepared long in advance and frozen, others can only be prepared a day or two ahead to save effort on the big day. It is important that you enjoy the occasion as much as your guests, so the more preparation you can do in advance the better. Always allow yourself time to dress up and relax. What is the point of giving a wonderful entertainment if you are a worn out wreck, before, during or after it?

Decide what you will prepare ahead and draw up the shopping list accordingly. Aim to finish cooking by lunch time of the day of the meal. You should have only last minute tasks to complete immediately before your guests arrive.

As for wine? The simple answer for a special meal is to serve a dry sparkling wine throughout. Another approach would be to go for a dry sherry to greet the guests. An Oloroso Secco would be excellent—not devastatingly dry, but by no means sweet—and this would be suitable to drink with the soup as well. Wine and soup are not good partners, except fortified wines like Sherry, Madeira or Port. For the mushroom parcels, a full flavoured Sancerre or a dry Chablis, and for the tofu pouches, a Claret or Burgundy would match the rich flavours. For pudding, an elegant sweet Sauternes, sweet Riesling or Doux Champagne. If your preference is for supermarket plonk, then go ahead. Wine is very much a subjective matter and the point is to choose something that pleases *you*. I like pink Champagne, a little over the top perhaps, but then so are seven course meals! Bon Appetit!

Peppered Cob Nuts

The peppery flavour really brings out the sweetness in the hazelnuts. They can be prepared up to a week in advance and stored in an airtight tin. They are so quick and easy, I prefer to roast them at the last minute and serve them hot from the oven. Choose whichever suits you best. I don't normally approve of added salt, but for a special occasion the rule can be set aside.

½ lb (225g) shelled cob nuts
2 tablespoons (30ml) olive or hazelnut oil
good pinch cayenne pepper
generous grinding of black peppercorns
generous sprinkling of sea or rock salt

Begin by giving the nuts a preliminary baking for 3 or 4 minutes spread on a shallow dish in a hot oven 425°F/220°C (gas mark 7). Put the roast nuts in a tea towel and rub them vigorously to remove most of the skins. While they are still hot, put them back in the dish and pour over the oil, turning the nuts to coat them, and return them to the oven, now reduced to a cool 325°F/170°C (gas mark 3) for a further 15 minutes. The nuts should taste dry and crisp. Sprinkle the hot nuts with salt and the two peppers, turning them well. If you intend to store them in a tin, allow them to cool completely first.

Green Almond Soup

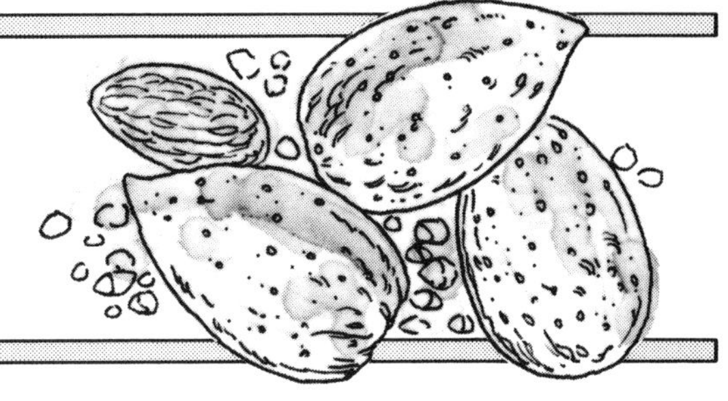

A subtly-flavoured soup with a lovely pale colour. Almonds impart creaminess though not a pronounced flavour. If you want to intensify the almond flavour, you could add a drop of real almond essence at the end of cooking, though I don't really think it's necessary.

1 large onion
1 oz (30g) butter
¾ lb (340g) green beans
1 parsley root or a small bundle of parsley stems or 1 small parsnip
blade of mace
2 teaspoons (10ml) ground coriander
¼ pint (140ml) medium dry Sherry
1½ pints (850ml) water
4 oz (115g) whole almonds
juice of 1 lemon

Roughly chop the onion and sweat gently in the butter with the beans, parsley root, mace and coriander for 10 minutes. Add the Sherry and ½ pint (285ml) water to the pan, bring to the boil, cover and simmer for 20 minutes. Grind the almonds (there's no need to blanch them) very finely in a nut mill or coffee grinder. (To clean away unwanted flavours, process a few cubes of dry bread).

When the vegetables are cooked, process them in a blender for 2 or 3 minutes until completely smooth. Return to the pan and add the remaining 1 pint (570ml) water and the finely ground almonds. Bring to the boil and simmer for a minute or two to cook the almond 'flour'. Season to taste with lemon juice.

The soup freezes well for up to 2 months (and probably longer!) or it can be made up to two days in advance and stored in the fridge—beyond 2 days there is a danger that the onion will begin to ferment. A few toasted flaked almonds and a swirl of cream would be a suitable garnish, or a little finely chopped parsley or green beans.

Mushroom Parcels served with Garlic Cream and Mangetout

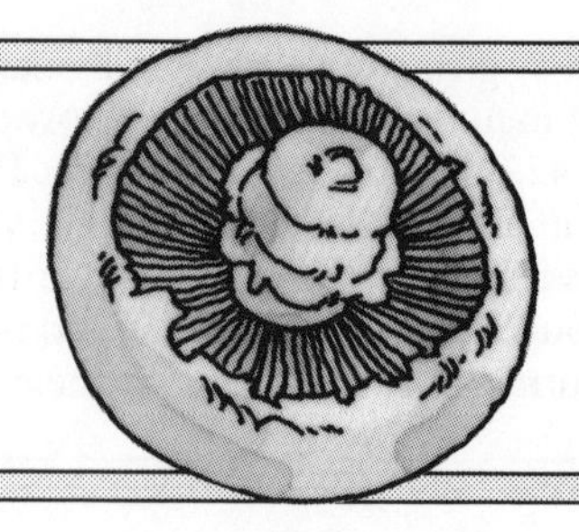

A wonderful combination of crisp pastry and strongly flavoured mushrooms with garlic cream. They look exceptionally attractive too. Prepare the parcels well in advance and freeze them if you prefer. If you can't get filo pastry, don't be daunted. Use very thinly rolled puff pastry instead.

4 sheets filo pastry or ¾ lb (340g) puff pastry
2 tablespoons (30ml) oil or melted butter if using filo pastry

Filling:
1 oz (30g) dried mushrooms
1 lb (455g) large field mushrooms
½ oz (15g) butter
3 bay leaves
generous glass red wine
1 tablespoon (15ml) soy sauce

Garlic cream:
½ good-sized head of garlic
8 oz (225g) fromage frais or yogurt

Garnish:
½ lb (225g) mangetout—fresh or frozen

Begin by preparing the mushroom filling. Soak the dried mushrooms in ½ pint (285ml) cold water for 30 minutes. Wash and finely chop the field mushrooms. They have a much better flavour than the small white sort. Put the butter, bay leaves and chopped field mushrooms in a pan over a low heat.

Once the juices begin to flow, add the dried mushrooms and their soaking liquid. A little sand may have accumulated at the bottom of the bowl so scoop out the mushrooms first, then pour in the liquid slowly, leaving any grit there may be in the bottom of the bowl. Add the soy sauce and red wine to the pan.

Turn the heat up to full and allow the juices in the pan to completely evaporate. This can take up to an hour, depending on the mushrooms, but the concentration of flavours is wonderful. Keep your eye on the pan for the final 3 or 4 minutes to avoid scorching. Don't be tempted to remove the pan from the heat too soon or you will be left with a soggy mixture that will make soggy parcels. Remove the bay leaves and allow the mixture to cool.

You can freeze the mixture on its own at this stage or store in the fridge for a day or two. The flavour actually improves with keeping!

Next, prepare the garlic cream. Don't bother to peel the garlic cloves, simply separate them from the bulb into individual cloves. Wrap them loosely in a piece of tinfoil and place in a warm oven 300°F/150°C (gas mark 2). Bake for 50–60 minutes until they are really soft and thoroughly well cooked. They will be full of flavour without being overwhelmingly garlicky. Slice the base off each clove and, using the back of a knife, push the soft garlic from its skin. Process the garlic in a blender with the fromage frais or yogurt until smooth and creamy. The cream does not take well to freezing, but it will store for up to a week in the fridge.

For the garnish, cook the peas in 1 inch (2.5cm) of fast boiling water for 3 minutes at the last moment before serving. They should retain all their crispness.

To assemble and serve the dish, lay the 4 sheets of filo pastry on top of each other, then cut into three across the width. Have to hand the mushroom filling and a bowl containing 2 tablespoons melted butter or olive oil and a pastry brush. Take one of the pastry sheets, brush it lightly with oil, then fold it in half and put a generous spoonful of filling in the centre. Draw up the pastry, and pinch and twist the neck of the parcel together. It should look something like a plump bouquet garni. Repeat until you have 12 parcels.

Bake the parcels in a moderately hot oven 375°F/190°C (gas mark 5) for 15–20 minutes until golden brown. This can all be done up to 24 hours in advance and the parcels flashed in a hot oven for 5 minutes just before serving, to warm them through. They also freeze well. If using puff pastry, roll it very thinly and cut into 12 approximately 6 inch (15cm) squares, then proceed as described earlier.

Serve the hot parcels on individual plates, sitting on a puddle of garlic cream at room temperature, with a fan of hot, crisp mangetout.

Water Melon Sorbet

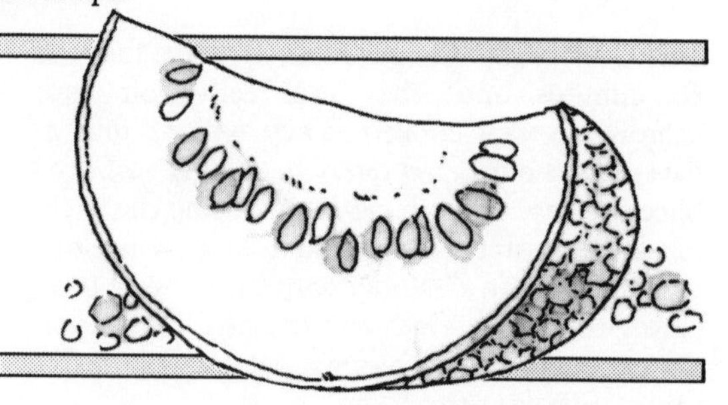

This light ice is the perfect way to refresh the palate. If you can't get orange flower water, try adding a couple of tablespoons (30ml) of Grand Marnier to bring up the flavour—because of the sweetness of the liqueur you could reduce the sugar by 1 oz (30g). Allow your guests to linger over the sorbet and enjoy the conversation. Don't be tempted to race them on to the next course.

¾ pint (425ml) water melon juice
6 oz (170g) white sugar (it gives a better colour)
juice ½ lemon
3 tablespoons (45ml) orange flower water—optional
1 egg white

Boil ¼ pint (140ml) melon juice with the sugar for 2–3 minutes until the sugar is completely dissolved. The easiest way to extract the juice is to squeeze the melon through a piece of muslin or the toe of a clean stocking. Stir the rest of the water melon juice (no pips!), orange flower water and lemon juice into the syrup and place in the freezer. I never set the temperature to extra cold and I always get perfect results.

When the mixture has frozen to a fairly firm mush, whisk it well with an electric mixer, and return to the freezer while you whisk the egg white until firm and peaky. Still using the electric mixer, whisk the egg white into the frozen mush and return the bowl to the freezer until properly frozen. The sorbet will keep in the freezer for up to 3 months.

Serve the sorbet on saucers, or in wine glasses or small glass dishes. Use two tablespoons, dipped frequently in warm water, to make attractive quenelle shapes or use an ice cream scoop. I make the shapes in advance and store them in the freezer ready to be popped on serving dishes at the appropriate moment. Allow at least 10 minutes resting time in the fridge before serving. This allows the flavour to develop.

Lord Liu An's Delight

Although the soya bean is reputed to have been an important food crop in China as far back as 2000 B.C., legend has it that tofu, a soya bean product, was not invented until around 200 B.C. The great and noble Chinese Lord Liu An, it is said, invented it to supplement the diet of Taoist monks who ate no animal flesh. Served with a tiny portion of wild rice and hot cherry tomatoes, this is a stunning dish and a little knowledge of the history of tofu adds extra spice!

3 blocks plain, firm tofu—approx 9 oz (225g) per block
3½-4oz (100g) fresh parsley
2 oz (55g) pine kernels
1 teaspoon (5ml) miso
3 tablespoons (45ml) soy sauce
1 tablespoon (15ml) oil for frying—perferably peanut

Use firm tofu, not the 'silken' kind which is best suited to creams, dips and shakes. Tofu has a high proportion of liquid, so to prepare the pouches for this dish you must begin by drying and pressing it. Wrap each block in 4 or 5 sheets of kitchen towel and place a weight (about 2 lb or 900g) on them for 5 minutes. The paper will be soaked, so discard it and repeat the process. At the end of the second pressing, wrap the tofu once more in paper or a clean tea towel and this time leave it to press for 1 to 6 hours, according to what best suits your schedule. I know it sounds fiddly, but it isn't really and your efforts will be well rewarded.

Wash the parsley and place it in a pan with no extra water. Turning it constantly, cook it over a high heat for 2–3 minutes until quite wilted but still bright green and with some firmness left. There should be no liquid at all. Allow it to cool, and chop finely. Combine the parsley and pine kernels with one teaspoon of miso. The stuffing is now ready.

Take the pressed tofu and, with a sharp, pointed knife, cut into one edge of each block to form a pouch. In meat eater's terms, it should be something like a Chicken Kiev fillet, ready to be filled. Pack each opening with stuffing. Pinch the edges shut and seal with cocktail sticks. Lay the pouches on a plate and pour a tablespoon (15ml) of naturally brewed soy sauce over each one. Allow to marinade, uncovered, for at least 30 minutes. You can prepare up to this point a day ahead if you wish. Fry the pouches for 6–7 minutes, turning them over halfway through. You are simply re-heating them, so don't be tempted to over-cook—there is nothing that needs cooking. Serve the pouches on a warmed plate with any marinade that remains or a simple sauce of 4 tablespoons (60ml) of tomato juice mixed with 2 tablespoons of soy sauce. Half or even a third of a pouch per person is ample. Remember that this is a seven course meal and portions should not be too large!

To Accompany Lord Liu An's Delight

Baked Cherry Tomatoes

18 cherry tomatoes or 12 small tomatoes
1 tablespoon (15ml) white wine

Cover the tomatoes with boiling water for half a minute, then peel their skins away. Place the tomatoes in a small dish with white wine, cover with tin foil and bake in a hot oven 450°F/220°C (gas mark 7) for 5 minutes immediately before serving.

Wild Rice

Wild rice isn't really rice at all—it's a grass seed! Just serve a tiny portion of this exotic grain with the tofu pouches. For a less extravagant approach, you could mix it with brown or white rice.

3 oz (85g) wild rice
½ pint (285ml) water

Rinse the wild rice and put it in a pan with ½ pint (285ml) water and bring to the boil. Simmer gently for 15–20 minutes. Drain and serve with a nut of butter and a squeeze of fresh lemon juice.

Opposite Nuts and Bolts (page 37) and Peanut and Wheatgerm Goodies (page 38).

Persimmon Pies with Honey Cream

The persimmon, which originated in Japan, must only be eaten when absolutely ripe, soft and pulpy, otherwise it tastes horrible! The sharon fruit, which looks identical, is a non-astringent development of the persimmon and doesn't suffer this drawback. If you can't find persimmons or sharon fruit, use fresh ripe peaches or kiwi fruit instead.

Pastry:
3 oz (85g) wholemeal flour
3 oz (85g) white flour
3 oz (85g) butter
2 oz (55g) icing sugar
1 large egg
drop real vanilla essence

Filling:
3–4 persimmons
2 teaspoons (10ml) cinnamon
juice ½ lemon
honey to taste
5 oz (140g) fromage frais or thick yogurt
5 oz (140g) crème fraîche

Opposite Almond and Apricot Cake (page 48), Arrowroot and Bay Leaf Custard Tart with Fresh Peaches (page 45) and a Date Castle (page 51).

Put the flours on a work surface—a marble slab is ideal. Make a well in the centre and put in the soft butter, sugar, egg and vanilla essence. Using the fingertips of one hand, work the butter, egg, sugar and essence together gradually drawing in the flour. When all is blended, work the paste with the heel of your hand two or three times to achieve a smooth finish. Wrap the ball in foil or cling film and leave to rest in the fridge for at least 30 minutes.

Roll thinly and line 6 individual tartlet tins or an 8 inch (20cm) flan ring. Don't use a ceramic flan dish as they invariably make pastry soggy. Prick the base with a fork to stop the pastry bubbling and line it with tin foil. Bake in a moderately hot oven 375°F/190°C (gas mark 5) for 10 minutes, remove the foil and bake for a further 5 minutes until the pastry is crisp and golden. Pâté sucrée, which is what this pastry is, will keep for at least a day if you wish to prepare it in advance.

To prepare the filling, wash and chop the fruit into small dice. Mix the fruit with the cinnamon and lemon juice, adding a little honey if you feel the mixture needs sweetening. Put the fruit to one side. Mix the thick yogurt or framage frais with the crème fraîche, sweetening them with a scant tablespoon (15ml) of honey. You could use whipped double cream instead.

Not more than 2 hours ahead, fill the tartlet cases with fruit and cover generously with honey cream. Refrigerate. If you are really out to impress, sprinkle the cream with brown sugar and flash the tartlet under a very hot grill for just long enough to melt the sugar without heating the fruit. Then garnish each one with a few redcurrants and a leaf of mint or sweet cicely as they go to the table. Un-grilled honey cream with a sprinkle of cinnamon looks perfectly pretty if you are feeling less adventurous.

Golden Honeycomb Nuggets

I always like to serve something sweet with coffee at the end of a meal. Chocolates can seem a little clichéd after a meal that was very special. My golden nuggets are simply good old fashioned cinder toffee cut into dainty pieces. The quantity I've given will ensure there's lots left over for the kids, but remember to tell them to brush their teeth afterwards!

2 oz (55g) brown sugar
4 oz (115g) golden syrup
2 teaspoons (10ml) bicarbonate of soda
2 oz (55g) finely chopped preserved ginger—optional

Boil the sugar and syrup together in a *large* pan until they are a rich golden colour. Add the chopped ginger if you are using it. While the mixture is still boiling, stir in the bicarbonate of soda. The contents of the pan will expand enormously, which is why it is essential to use a large one! Pour the mixture into a well greased Swiss-roll tin and leave to cool. When it is firm, but not set, loosen the edges with a knife and tip it out. You can cut it into small nuggets at this stage or, if it has become too hard, simply break it into smallish pieces. It will store in an airtight tin for up to 2 weeks.

Entertaining in Simpler Vein

This meal is very easy to cope with, but retains the characteristics of the grand menu. The basic watch points and principles remain the same: prepare the food well in advance, lay the table, have coffee cups, etc. all to hand. There is little point in cooking ahead then spending hours in the kitchen pulling out cupboards, frantically searching for a missing saucer or some such. The most common lament from the cook is 'everyone but me had a wonderful time—I was too frazzled and exhausted to relax or enjoy myself'. This is the kind of meal that enables you to remain unfrazzled and allows plenty of time for choosing which socks or earrings to wear on the night. Almost as important a consideration as what goes on the menu!

A dish of black olives, preferably Greek Calamata olives with their rich, smooth flavour, and a glass of tangy, chilled Manzanilla would make an excellent aperitif. The melon with ginger wine is best unaccompanied. With the roulade, serve a light red wine, perhaps a Beaujolais-Villages or a Loire red, or, if you prefer white wines, try a light, fairly dry Muscadet or a dry white Burgundy, which has rather more body. Choosing wine for an iced pudding is always a problem. The easiest solution is to opt for a sparkling wine. If you are feeling extravagant, serve Champagne, but a well chilled Asti Spumante would be my choice. English farmhouse cheeses call for a robust Claret. A completely different approach would be to invest in a flagon of the very best, smooth, dry farmhouse cider. Or you could go for Vinho Verde throughout. It has a slight sparkle or *pétillance*, is refreshingly light, and low in alcohol. It is really a matter of how seriously you want to treat the occasion. Choose the option that you will be comfortable with.

Charentais Melon Perfumed with Ginger Wine

A simple and elegant start to any meal. The little Charentais melons should be served lightly chilled. The best way to check for ripeness is to sniff them. There should be a fragrant sweetness and, to double check, the flesh should give slightly when pressed at the stalk end. If you have any water melon ice (see previous menu) left over, try filling a scooped out melon with a little for an excellent starter or light pudding on a hot summer day. It could also be filled with fresh raspberries, a fruit that has a great affinity with melons.

1 small Charentais melon per person or ½ a larger one
¼-½ pint (140-285ml) green ginger wine

Slice the tops off the melons and scoop out and discard the seeds (or wash and dry them for the kids to thread into bracelets and necklets). Put the melons in the fridge until required for serving. Add two or three tablespoons (30–45ml) of ginger wine to each melon just before serving.

Roulade of Calabrese with Classic Orange Sauce

Roulades have become a classic in the vegetarian repertoire. They come in innumerable forms and guises, and this one is, I think, particularly elegant. You could experiment with the basic recipe by using different nuts, trying vegetables such as spinach, asparagus, a ragoût of red peppers or celery with apple for instance, or swap the sauce. The light soufflé mixture is always reliable and reheats well. Accompanied by a dish of creamy, oven crisped potatoes and artichoke bottoms filled with lightly cooked carrots, this is a substantial and delicious main course.

Roulade:
6 oz (170g) pecans
4 large eggs separated + 1 extra egg white
2 tablespoons (30ml) chopped parsley
¾ lb (340g) steamed calabrese (broccoli) florets
4 oz (115g) roughly chopped pistachios

Sauce:
4 tablespoons (60ml) cide vinegar
3 bay leaves
10 black peppercorns
3 egg yolks
finely grated peel of 1 small orange, and its juice
6 oz (170g) butter
pinch freshly grated nutmeg

Line and butter a Swiss-roll tin. Grind 4 oz (115g) of the pecans in a nut mill or coffee grinder until finely ground. Beat the separated egg yolks and finely chopped parsley together and stir in the ground nuts. Whisk the egg whites until firm and peaky, and carefully fold them into the egg yolk mixture. Pour the mixture into the prepared tin and bake in a fairly hot oven 400°F/200°C (gas mark 6) for 10–15 minutes until firm to touch in the centre. Lay a piece of greaseproof paper on a clean, damp tea towel. Turn the roulade out onto the paper, peel away the lining paper and carefully roll it up, Swiss-roll style. Cool it, loosely rolled, while you prepare the sauce.

Boil the cider vinegar with bay leaves and peppercorns in a small pan until reduced to one tablespoon (15ml). Place the egg yolks, finely grated peel of the orange and nutmeg in a liquidizer goblet. Add the butter to the reduced vinegar and melt it gently, until it is just liquid. Start the liquidizer running and very, very, slowly, pour in a thin, steady stream of melted butter. Don't hurry or the mixture will curdle. Allow the machine a few minutes rest half way through if it seems to be struggling. This method is far easier than whisking by hand and is totally reliable as long as you proceed slowly. Add the orange juice last.

Gently unroll the roulade and spread it with about one third of the sauce. Reserve a few small florets of the steamed calabrese for garnishing. Fill the roll with the rest. Sprinkle with half the pistachio nuts and remaining pecans. Carefully re-roll and cover the roulade with tin foil. This can be done 3 or 4 hours before the meal. 5 minutes before serving, put it in a hot oven 425°F/220°C (gas mark 7) to warm through. Slightly warm the sauce—it must not boil—and pour over the re-heated roulade. Scatter the top with the reserved calabrese and nuts. Serve immediately.

To Accompany the Roulade

Potatoes Dauphinoise

The culinarily correct version of this dish contains Gruyère cheese, but on this occasion I have decided to omit it. I tend not to peel the potatoes, though this is a matter of personal choice.

2 lb (900g) potatoes
½ pint (285ml) single cream
¼ pint (140ml) milk
1 oz (30g) butter
black pepper

Wash the potatoes and slice them very thinly. Grease a shallow oven proof dish with a little of the butter. Arrange the potatoes in layers in the dish, peppering each layer as you go. Pour the cream and milk over the potatoes and dot the top with the remaining butter. Cover closely with foil or greaseproof paper and bake in a moderate oven 350°F/180°C (gas mark 4) for 1½ hours. This dish can be assembled in the afternoon and put in to bake just before your guests arrive.

Artichoke Cups with Herbed Carrots

Use tinned artichoke bottoms unless you have plenty of time to prepare fresh ones. Tinned ones really don't taste bad at all, provided you rinse them well—one of the few vegetables that seem to survive being tinned. I allow two 15 oz (425g) tins for 6 people, but one is probably enough if you are economizing. The carrots can be prepared the day before the meal. I find their sweetness goes very well with the artichokes.

¾ lb (340g) carrots
½ oz (15g) butter
2 strips thinly pared lemon rind
½ teaspoon (2.5ml) sugar
½ teaspoon (2.5ml) dried thyme or a good sized sprig of fresh thyme
1 or 2 x 15 oz (425g) tins artichoke bottoms

Peel and grate the carrots. Cook them over a moderate heat with all the ingredients except the artichoke bottoms, for about 7–8 minutes, until cooked but with a little crispness remaining. Remove the lemon rind and thyme sprig, if you used one. The carrots can be put on one side at this stage, until required for serving.

To assemble, simply warm the artichoke bottoms, re-heat the herbed carrots and 'top the bottoms' with a generous quantity of carrots.

Paskha Cassata

This is a glorious combination of cultures. Somewhere between a Paskha, a Russian Easter treat made with cream cheese and candied fruits, and a traditional Sicilian Mothering Sunday 'cake', a cassata of ricotta cheese and candied fruit, with just a hint of Florence's famous, Duomo-like, Zuccotto pudding. The final effect is quite rich, but because it is made with cottage cheese and sour cream (or smetana), it is relatively low in fat. For those who have cast caution to the wind, a generous helping of cream (or crème fraîche for the health conscious) over a portion of Paskha Cassata is nothing less than sublime. This Paskha Cassata should be prepared at least 24 hours in advance, to allow the flavours to blend and develop.

¾ lb (340g) plain cake—sponge or madeira is best
1 lb (455g) cottage cheese
5 oz (140ml) sour cream or smetana
3 tablespoons (45ml) Marsala or sweet Sherry
2 oz (55g) each glacé pineapple, orange and apricot
2 oz (55g) raisins
2 oz (55g) plain chocolate

Slice the cake into approximately ½ inch (1.25cm) slices. Cut the slices diagonally across the middle to make triangular shapes, and use to neatly line a 2½ pint (1.5 litre) bowl. Reserve enough cake to cover the filling later. If you feel nervous about turning the pudding out successfully, line the bowl with clingfilm first for guaranteed turn-out-ability. Process the drained cottage cheese in a blender for a few seconds until it is smooth. Pour the cottage cheese into a bowl and add the sour cream or smetana, Marsala, finely chopped glacé fruits, raisins and coarsely grated chocolate. Stir it well. Pour the mixture into the lined bowl and cover it with the reserved slices of cake. Don't worry if it seems a little runny, it will firm up. Cover with tin foil and top with a small plate. Leave at room temperature for at least a day to develop a smooth flavour and firm texture. To serve it, tip it out onto a plate and cut a slice for each guest. Serve it plain, or with cream, or chocolate sauce—if your arteries can take it!

An English Cheese Board with Apples and Pears

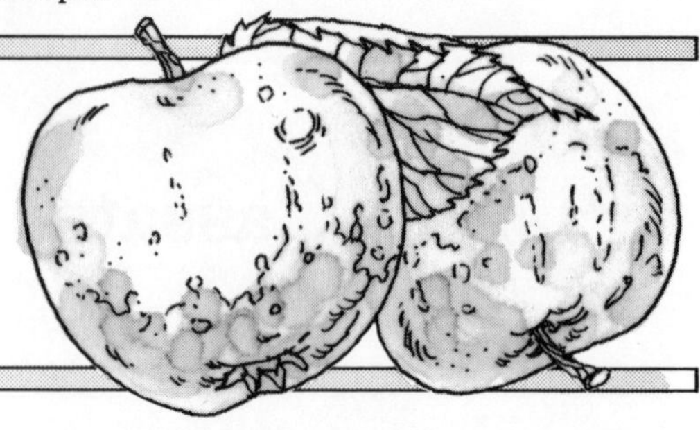

I don't think it would be useful to suggest which cheeses to serve. The point is to buy the best which is available in your area and serve them at room temperature. Most cheeses are made with rennet derived from animals. Some vegetarians prefer to eat only cheeses made with vegetable rennet and, happily, there is an increasing variety of excellent vegetable rennet cheeses available. However, the plastic, fatty lumps described as 'vegetarian cheddar' are usually flavourless and best left on the shelf to encourage shops to stock the many vegetarian cheeses that are worth eating! Cheeses are often not described as being 'rennet-free' or 'made with vegetable rennet' even though they are. Find a good cheesemonger and ask for advice. There are several excellent vegetarian goat's cheeses widely available. Farmhouses cheeses to look out for include Botton from North Yorks, Bonchester from the Scottish borders, Pencarreg from West Wales and Yarg, a Cornish cheese. Jewish Kosher cheeses are also vegetarian. They are made with vegetable rennet in order to conform to the strict dietary rules of Kashrut, and are another avenue worth investigation for the cheese-aholic. It is my opinion that the vegan (who eats no animal products) should simply accept that cheese is not on their agenda. Sava, *the so called 'nut cheese' is quite disgusting! A vegan could, however, try marinaded or smoked tofu if the desire for a 'cheese board' is irresistible.*

Crisp English apples and sweet pears are the perfect match for good, unpasteurized, farmhouse cheese. Allow about 2–3 oz (55g–85g) of cheese per person. I think cheeses are fine on their own. I rarely serve crackers and never butter, but that is a matter you should decide for yourself.

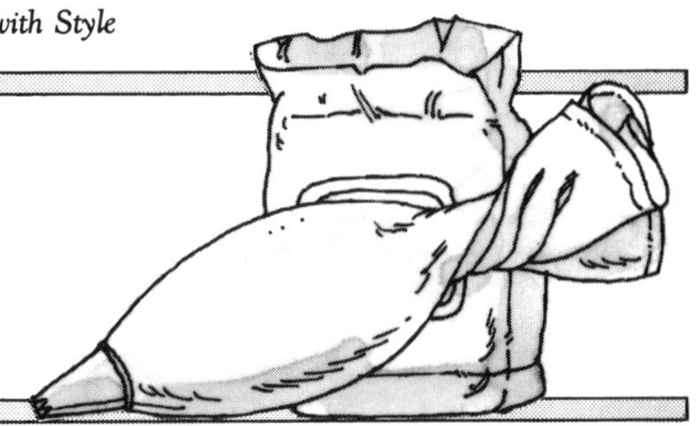

Old Fashioned Peppermint Creams

There is something very pleasant about offering guests home made sweets at the end of a meal. Nothing could be simpler than these peppermint creams. You could turn them into coffee creams by using coffee essence instead of peppermint. They must dry out for at least 12, and preferably, 24 hours, so make them well ahead. Stored in an air-tight tin, they will keep for at least a week or two. Serve them on a pretty dish and try not to eat too many—after all, they are almost pure sugar.

1 egg white
½ lb (225g) icing sugar
few drops real peppermint essence

Whisk the egg white until stiff and peaky. Sift the icing sugar onto the egg white and work the two together. I use my fingers, though a wooden spoon would do. Add two drops of peppermint essence and work that in. Taste the mixture. If you feel it isn't strong enough, add another drop and mix that in. I find three drops is just about right, but it will depend on the essence. Only use a pure oil of peppermint essence. The flavoured, inexpensive concoctions are exactly that: cheap and nasty. Roll the paste out, using a little extra icing sugar, and stamp out shapes if you have a set of small cutters or use a knife to cut dainty diamonds. Put the creams on a wire rack to dry for at least 12 hours.

A Gourmet Meal in a Hurry

Draw up your shopping list, shop and get the cooking over with as early as possible, so you can spend the rest of your time on yourself. Good food is important, but so is being able to enjoy an evening with your guests. It is the little touches—a pretty table, attractive food and a relaxed you, that make all the difference.

If you are totally rushed off your feet, you could miss out the cucumber terrines (though it would be a pity) and even (oh! could you really?) swap the leek and pear strudel for a dish of bought spaghetti or tagliatelle with bought tomato or cream sauce, adding a generous sprinkling of toasted, slivered almonds and a good salad. This could be something like a base of crisp lettuce, mixed with a little red radicchio, some curly endive and perhaps a chopping of fresh coriander if you can get it, and/or some slivers of green pepper. Dress it with two or three tablespoons (30-45ml) of aromatic walnut oil and a teaspoon (5ml) of lemon juice. Rose Water Mousse is so easy, so quick and so delicious that even the busiest cook should be able to fit it in. The cheese board and chocolates are simply a matter of buying the best in your area—no cooking involved, but don't stint the presentation. Food should be enjoyed as much by the eye as by the palate.

Asparagus and Orange Soup

1 small onion
½ oz (15g) butter
½ teaspoon (2.5ml) freshly grated nutmeg
1 large orange
2 x 12 oz (340g) tins green asparagus
1½ pints (850ml) skimmed milk
2 tablespoons (30ml) lemon juice

Chop the onion and fry in the butter, with the nutmeg, until soft. Scrub the orange well and, using a potato peeler, thinly peel half the rind into long strips. Add all but two of the orange peel strips to the frying onion. Cut the remaining strips of rind into very fine matchsticks, place them in a small bowl and cover with boiling water. Leave them to soak while you finish preparing the soup.

Squeeze the juice from the peeled orange and place it, together with the drained asparagus, in a liquidizer. When the onion and peel is softened, add to the liquidizer with ½ pint (285ml) milk. Process until smooth. Tip the contents of the liquidizer back in the pan and add the remaining pint (570ml) of milk and the lemon juice. The soup is now ready simply to be heated when you want to serve it.

Drain the peel matchsticks and wrap them in a piece of kitchen paper until you are ready to scatter a little into the middle of each bowl of soup, with a scraping of nutmeg, as it goes to the table.

Cucumber Terrine

These individual terrines should be shaped in a neat round. A plain scone cutter 2 inches (5cm) in diameter is perfect. Failing that, use two tablespoons to form neat shapes—two per serving.

12 oz (340g) smoked tofu
10 oz (285ml) sour cream
2 teaspoons (10ml) dried dill
(4 tablespoons (60ml) fresh)
good pinch black pepper

Garnish:
1 lemon
2-3 tablespoons (30-45ml) green or pink peppercorns
few sprigs fresh dill, if possible
¼ unpeeled cucumber, very finely sliced

Begin by drying the tofu on kitchen roll, then grate it into a bowl. Use the side of the grater that you would normally use for cheese. The sour cream *must* be thick. If it isn't, put it into a small bowl, add a tablespoon (15ml) of fresh lemon juice (not allowed for in the recipe) and leave it in a warm place for a least an hour—overnight if you have the time to spare. It will thicken up beautifully. Stir 6 tablespoons (90ml) of sour cream, together with the dill and black pepper, into the grated tofu and mix.

Place the scone cutter slightly to one side on a small plate. Fill the mould almost to the top with the tofu mixture. Smooth it over and leave a gap of a bit more than ¼ inch (½ cm) at the top. Press the tofu gently down to make a good firm shape. Fill the gap at the top of the mould with sour cream, smoothing it neatly with a knife. Run the knife around the inside of the mould to help loosen the contents, then gently lift the mould up to leave behind a neatly shaped terrine. Repeat this process until you have 6 terrines on small plates. If you are shaping the mixture with tablespoons, lay the shapes on a bed of the sour cream you would otherwise have used to top the moulds.

Garnishing is an important element in this dish. It doesn't take long once you have done the first one, so don't hurry that one and you will be surprised how quickly you cope with the rest. Lay a few small pieces of cucumber on the top of the first terrine with 5 or 6 peppercorns in the centre. Garnish the terrines with fresh dill or chervil if you can get it. Lay a fan of cucumber slices on the plate and add a thin wedge of lemon. Repeat with all the terrines. Store them in the fridge until you are ready to serve them. They can be prepared up to 5 or 6 hours in advance. I find it takes me about 20 minutes to produce 6 little terrines. Serve with hot melba toast or warm wholemeal rolls. I don't think it is necessary to offer butter.

Leek and Pear Strudel with Cider Sauce

This is the kind of dish that makes a cook's reputation, despite the fact that it is actually very easy. It freezes well, so perhaps you could make a double batch? If you can't get filo pastry, use ready made puff pastry or instant bread mix to enclose the filling.

6 oz (170g) buckwheat—unroasted
1 tablespoon (15ml) shoyu
1 rounded tablespoon (20ml) plum or red currant or gooseberry jam
2 lb (900g) leeks
¾ lb (340g) hard pears—Conference for preference
½ oz (15g) butter
4 tablespoon (60ml) dry cider —dry farmhouse for preference
1 teaspoon (5ml) cider or rice vinegar
6 sheets (225g) filo pastry
2 tablespoons (30ml) poppy seeds
1 oz (30g) melted butter
2 tablespoons (30ml) olive oil

Place the buckwheat, shoyu and jam in a large pan that has a tight fitting lid—you'll be adding the leeks and pears later so you need the space. Add 12 fl oz (340ml) water, mix in the jam and shoyu and bring to the boil. Like rice, buckwheat grains should not be stirred as they cook or they become sticky. Put the lid on the pan and simmer for 15 minutes.

Meanwhile, finely slice the cleaned leeks and peel and chop the pears. Place 4 oz (115g) of chopped leeks and one third of the pears in a separate pan with ½ oz (15g) butter and the dry cider—you could use white wine instead—cover with a lid and simmer very gently until soft. This will form the basis of the sauce.

When the buckwheat has simmered for 15 minutes, add the uncooked leeks and pears and replace the lid. Allow the mixture to steam for another 15 minutes. You will need to shake the pan once or twice during cooking. You are aiming for a fairly dry mixture with a little bite left in the vegetables. This is the strudel filling.

When the pear and leek combination for the sauce is soft, put it in a liquidizer with the cider or rice vinegar (much less acidic than other vinegars) and process until smooth. This makes a very thick sauce. Thin it by adding just a little less than ¼ pint (140ml) cold water or cider. Return the mixture to the pan until required for serving.

To assemble the strudel, put the olive oil and butter in a small dish and have to hand a pastry brush. Unroll the filo and work fairly quickly—filo becomes brittle, drying out the longer it is exposed to air. Cover it with a damp tea towel if you work slowly, or if you have to leave it for any reason. Oil a baking sheet and lay the first piece of pastry on it. Oil that sheet of pastry and lay the next one on top of it. Continue until all six sheets of the filo are on the baking sheet. Tip the filling onto the pastry, keeping it in one neat, fat, sausage shape. Leave an inch or 'two of pastry at each end for folding in. Fold the ends of the pastry, then roll it up to enclose the filling. Ensure the join is underneath for baking. The top must be well oiled, then sprinkle thickly with poppy seeds. If you want the strudel to look really spectacular, take an extra sheet of filo, scrunch it up like a silk scarf and lay it on top of the roll, then oil it and scatter the seeds on the frilly pastry. (If you are intending to freeze the strudel, this is the stage at which it should be frozen). Bake in a moderately hot oven 375°F/190°C (gas mark 5) for 30 minutes (allow longer if cooking from frozen). The 'frill' will need a foil covering after about 15 minutes to avoid scorching. If you use puff pastry or bread mix instead of filo, it is simply a matter of wrapping the filling in your chosen medium and baking accordingly.

Serve with warmed cider sauce and enjoy the praise. The strudel could be prepared and baked several hours in advance and re-heated for serving, but it does taste best if the pastry is freshly baked. Accompany with broad beans, broccoli, carrots or courgettes and boiled potatoes with a generous sprinkling of finely chopped parsley, chervil or chives.

Rose Water Mousse with Brandy Snaps

Buy the best quality brandy snaps or almond macaroons you can to compliment this aromatic old recipe. Use real rose water rather than merely 'flavoured' if possible. Asian, Greek or Turkish shops are usually the best sources of good quality flower water. Try the local chemist only at the last resort.

2 oz (55g) brown rice
½ pint (285ml) double cream
½ pint (285ml) milk
1 teaspoon (5ml) ground cinnamon
3 eggs—separated
1½ tablespoons (22.5ml) runny honey
6 tablespoons (90ml) rose water
1 rosy pomegranate

Place the brown rice in a coffee grinder and process till very fine. Put the ground rice in a pan together with the cream, milk, and cinnamon. Bring gently to the boil, stirring continuously, and cook for 3 or 4 minutes. Separate the eggs and whisk the yolks into the rice. Beat the honey and rose water into the cream. Leave the mixture, tightly covered in order to stop a skin developing, to cool.

When the cream is quite cold, whisk the egg whites until they are stiff and peaky and fold them into the cream. The mixture is rich, so a small quantity will be sufficient for each guest. Serve it in little chocolate pots or small wine glasses sitting on doily covered tea plates with two or three of your bought biscuits. Take the seeds from the pomegranate and liberally sprinkle the top of each creamy mousse with the glistening, scarlet seeds. I think you can only agree that they ate remarkably well in the 16th century. They called this delicious concoction *Spanish pap*—I prefer my name!

For those who want a less rich mixture, the cream could be omitted altogether and skimmed milk used instead. Vegans could try the basic quantities given, but using bean milk or water and omitting the eggs. Of course the mousse effect will be lacking, but the mixture is still very good, particularly if there are a few pistachios nestling among the pomegranate seeds. If making the less rich version, increase the liquid to 1½ pints (850ml), the ground rice to 2½ oz (70g) and increase the flavourings accordingly, otherwise you may feel there isn't enough to satisfy your guests' appetities—hardly a problem with the richer mixture!

The Cheese Board

Buy the best you can—as usual really—by which I mean farmhouse cheeses made with unpasteurised milk. Serve the cheeses at room temperature, not straight from the fridge. If you are fortunate enough to have access to a vine, cheeses look superb laid on a bed of fresh leaves. Failing fresh leaves, a good marble or china plate or even a straw mat will add to the aesthetic appeal of your selection. Three or four cheeses would be fine. As a rough guide, allow 2–3 oz (55–85g) per person. Serve the cheeses with a basket of dried fruits and nuts for nibbling. I would not bother with crackers and I never serve butter with cheese (it is fatty enough!). Line the fruit and nut basket with vine leaves, a napkin or paper doily. Lay out the cheese board and its accompaniments, as well as plates and knives, as you prepare the rest of the food. The more you prepare early, the less time you will need to spend in the kitchen once the guests have arrived.

Chocolates and Coffee

The coffee must be hot, strong and plentiful. Serve your bought sweets on a doily covered teaplate or saucer. Chocolate truffles are one of the favourites at my table. Set them out early and leave them in the fridge. If your guests don't want coffeee, try Rose Pouchong, a classic China tea, low in tannin and perfumed with rose petals, for a stylish end to a deliciously stylish meal.

5.
Branching Out

This chapter is about expanding culinary horizons. Part of the fun of vegetarian cooking is that all the boring old conventions are left behind. Red wine with meat, white wine with fish and turkey for Christmas all become irrelevant. It does indeed take a little while to cast off the conventions altogether and acquire a repertoire of dishes that suit your needs. But after the initial effort, you'll be delighted by a new and broader expertise.

What to cook for dinner? It is so much simpler, for the new vegetarian to think of meat substitute and two veg than cope with the freedom of vegetarian cookery. In fact, a new approach is required. I feel it is much easier to come to grips with new ingredients and ideas right from the start. I wonder how many good intentions to try a vegetarian diet have stumbled and finally collapsed under endless plates of stodge and rissoles that take hours to prepare only to crumble to dust when you cook them! This is where high protein, low bulk, easy to eat foods like tofu and sea vegetables come in—they seem to me so much more worthwhile than mountains of nuts and brown rice, and a lot less fattening too!

Try new ingredients bravely and have the courage of your own convictions. If you find something unpleasant, don't use it again for a few weeks. Then try it once more, and if you still don't like whatever it is, abandon it for a few months. Our palates and minds are slow to adjust to new foods (not to mention our digestive systems!), so take it slowly. After months of finding change difficult, one day you will discover it has all fallen into place and you didn't even notice!

The chapter on Children's Treats covers the basics on nutrition, so I won't go into that here, except to remind you not to worry about getting enough protein—you would have to work quite hard to be short of it!

All the recipes in this chapter are for 4 unless stated otherwise.

Stocking Up

I have compiled a short list of some of the ingredients that a vegetarian store cupboard should contain to make cooking easy and varied. Some of the more unusual items can be a little difficult to obtain, so it is worth stocking up when you can. I am a great believer in giving positive encouragement to shops to widen their range of goods. Don't be fobbed off with that old chestnut 'There's no call for it'. *You* just called for it and maybe one or two of your friends did too, so how can there be no call? If the shop is good enough to buy in a new product in response to your requests, then congratulate them on their pioneering spirit and become a regular customer. It isn't a matter of nagging, more gentle persuasion together with praise and extra custom in return for their efforts.

Buckwheat

Buckwheat is also known as Kasha or Saracen corn. It isn't actually a grain as you may think. Like wild rice, it is a grass. Buckwheat groats are a gluten-free, protein-rich food, high in B vitamins and iron, and sold both plain and ready roasted. Buy the plain sort as it is slightly cheaper and it only takes a few minutes to roast it yourself: place the grains in a pan and hold them over a slow heat for 4–5 minutes. They will soon develop a lovely nutty smell and brown colour. You can also roast them with a little oil in the pan if you prefer. Soba, Japanese spaghetti, is made with buckwheat flour. It is very light, making a pleasant change from traditional durum wheat pasta, and is also gluten-free.

Cider Vinegar

Cider vinegar is reputed to have all manner of properties. It is said to aid digestion, cure a cold, relieve muscle cramp, disperse bruises and a host of other things. I can't swear to its curative properties, but I do know it is less acidic than other vinegars and is one of the best salt substitutes available. Rice vinegar is another mild vinegar excellent for cooking, but usually only specialist Chinese or Japanese shops stock it so few cooks will have access to it. Whenever possible, buy cider vinegar made from organically grown apples, that is to say cider apples grown without the use of pesticides and other potentially harmful chemicals. I firmly believe that we should aim to reduce the toxic load our bodies must cope with whenever possible.

Gelling Agents

There are two sea vegetable gelling agents, each of which gives a slightly different set.

Agar agar is the proper name, but I'm among friends, so let's just call it agar. Agar is used as the vegetable equivalent of animal-based gelatine. It does not have such a splendidly wobbly set as gelatine, but the way round that is to serve the jelly cut into small pieces. Agar comes in two readily available forms, a bland, fine powder, or tiny, flavourless flakes. The flakes are formed by a long process of drying in a hot sun by day and freezing overnight. This breaks down the tough, unpleasant tasting sea vegetable in a gentle and natural way, without the need for any chemicals. The powder, on the other hand, is made much more quickly with the aid of sulphuric acid, bleaches and dyes, so, if possible, buy the flakes. The setting strength of agar depends on the acidity of the food being used. Acid food (lemons, rhubarb, pineapples) need more agar than something alkaline like bananas or almonds. But this does not present a problem because it is easy to check the set of an agar mix. Test it as you would test the set of jam. Drop a little hot agar mixture onto a plate. If it gels as it cools, you know the mixture is satisfactory, if not, then simply add a little extra agar, re-boil, re-test and there you are. If a pan of jelly sets before you get round to using it, just heat to melt it again—there will be no ill effects. 1 level teaspoon (5ml) of agar powder or 1 rounded tablespoon (20ml) of flakes will set ½ pint (285ml) liquid. If you use the powder, mix it with a little cold liquid before adding it to the main body to avoid lumps.

Carragheen also called Irish moss, is used to give a light, soft, mousse-like set. The Irish have used it for centuries to set a traditional milk pudding generally served with whisky sauce, as a cure for bronchial complaints (it is rich in vitamin A), and as a soup thickener. Some like it lightly boiled, to eat as a vegetable, but I can't say I am fond of it this way. On the other hand, I find a milk or chocolate mousse set with carragheen delicious. Add a tablespoon (15–30ml) or two to any type of soup you are preparing to give a smooth, rich texture. The flavour of carragheen is so subtle it blends with sweet or savoury.

Geska

Geska is a hard cheese made from skimmed cow's milk, it contains no animal rennet. Its blue green colour is derived from the herb 'blue meliot' which also gives it its distinctive flavour. Geska is a good substitute for Parmesan cheese.

Gram Flour

Gram flour, chick pea flour, garbanzo flour and besan flour are all names for the same thing: flour made from ground chick peas. Chick pea flour is rich in protein, B vitamins and minerals, and is gluten-free. It is available in Greek, Spanish and Asian shops as well as most health food shops. It makes splendid batters, pancakes, and a sort of thick omelette with the need for eggs. In fact it can be used like egg for its binding properties.

Oils

I prefer to use oils which fall into the category known as mono-unsaturates. This means that they are in the middle range, neither saturates nor poly-unsaturates. I know the current fashion is for poly-unsaturates, but it is a modern fad I do not subscribe to. I prefer to take a middle course. Mono-unsaturates are stable oils, unlike poly-unsaturates, and can be described as the oils of antiquity, as they've been used since the earliest times. When possible, choose cold pressed oils. Oils extracted at high temperatures with harsh chemical solvents are not my idea of a healthy product. Oil should be stored in a cool, dark place and not kept for longer than three or four months or it has a tendency to become rancid. The following oils are all high in mono-unsaturates.

Peanut (Groundnut) Oil. Almost flavourless and extremely light, leaving food dry and crisp. Use it for deep frying.

Olive Oil. Ideal for frying onions, garlic etc., for stews as well as making salad dressings. Greek Calamata olive oil is delicious and not too heavy. A good alternative would be Italian Lucca olive oil. As a general rule, the darker the oil, the stronger the flavour.

Sesame Oil. A delicious, powerfully flavoured oil. Use sparingly in stir-frys, salad dressings and dipping sauce for tempura vegetables. Only buy sesame oil that is richly dark. Some varieties have been processed to remove the flavour (goodness knows why!), and are quite pale in colour so not difficult to avoid.

Hazelnut and Walnut Oils. Both have a strong nutty flavour. They are the aristocrats of the salad dressing world. Such oils tend not to be used for other purposes because they are expensive and their flavour is best appreciated when used simply. An avocado served with walnut oil and just a drop of lemon juice lifts avocado vinaigrette from the banal to the sublime. Try it and you'll see what I mean!

Miso

Miso is a paste made by fermenting soya beans, rice or barley, salt and water with a mould starter for up to two years. It is used as a richly flavoured stock base, and is, in my opinion, vastly superior to any of the yeast extracts. Use it in soups, stews, casseroles, gravy, sauces and pie fillings, or mix it with an equal quanitity of ground walnuts or sesame seeds for a highly nutritious sandwich filling. The enzymes present in miso aid digestion and, it is thought, help rebuild the damaged villi of those suffering from coeliac disease. Miso contains vitamin B_{12}, rarely found in the vegetable world, as well as calcium and iron. To get the full benefit of its enzymes, miso should be added at the end of cooking if possible. It is usually sold in vacuum sealed packets or screw top jars. Stock up with as much as you like because it will keep indefinitely in the fridge.

Soy Sauce

What is the difference between soy sauce and shoyu? Nothing! Shoyu is just a fancy name some people prefer to use. Some soy sauce is really nothing more than a nasty mixture of chemicals, mostly monosodium glutamate and caramel, both of which have long been regarded with suspicion by health experts. Look for 'naturally brewed' soy sauce, and sadly, expect to pay a lot more than for the chemical cocktail variety. A good soy sauce is worth every penny, though I have found some expensive health food shop brands taste suspiciously thin, so price alone is no guide. *Kikkoman's Naturally Brewed* is the best variety in my opinion. It contains nothing more than water, soya beans, wheat and salt. Tamari looks and tastes identical to soy sauce but is made without wheat. It is therefore the natural alternative to soy sauce for those avoiding gluten. Soy sauce and Tamari keep indefinitely.

Sea Vegetables

There are many varieties of sea vegetables (sounds so much better than seaweed!). They really do deserve to be called 'health foods'. They all contain good supplies of protein as well as vitamins A, B and C and are a rich source of minerals. I have used only the mild flavoured varieties in the recipes for this chapter—the strong flavours of some varieties can be a bit of an acquired taste. Sea vegetables are sold dried, usually in quantities from ¼ oz (10g) up to around 4 oz (115g). As they are not always easy to find, it is worth stocking up when you find a supplier. The packets keep well for a least 6 months, but remember to keep them dry, especially once opened. With some of the better quality sea vegetables, you will discover a little bag of crystals included in the packet. This not a free gift of spices—the crystals keep the vegetables dry and are not for eating!

Arame is a mild, sweetly nutty sea vegetable, which has been used in Japan for over 1000 years. It is related to kombu and is particularly rich in calcium and iodine and contains good supplies of potassium. It is a traditional Japanese cure for womb related problems as well as high blood pressure. The finely slivered threads of arame generally need to be soaked in cold water for 10–15 minutes before use. On soaking, the strands will double in size, so bear this in mind when you are deciding how much to use. The crisp, deep fried sea vegetable you may find in Japanese and Chinese restaurants is usually arame. Give your plants the soaking water if you are not using it as stock—they will appreciate the minerals.

Dabberlocks. A sea vegetable with even more names than most. Sweet kombu, honey kombu, sea lettuce, tangle, gruaigean, sugar wrack, poor man's weatherglass or just plain dabberlocks—

take your pick! It is related to the main kombu group of sea vegetables, but is much finer and sweeter than the more commonly available kombu. It has a lovely mild flavour that will please all but the most closed minds (sea vegetables do tend to bring out the worst!). Use it in soups and stews (use around ½–1 oz (15–30g) in a stew for 4–6) or soak in cold water for 10 minutes, drain and use as a salad ingredient with a good oil and vinegar dressing.

Kombu is one of the most commonly available sea vegetables. It comes in strips about 2 inches (5cm) by 6 inches (15cm). Kombu is a traditional Japanese remedy for colitis as it is thought, like miso, to strengthen the colon and help the body eliminate toxins. It is also high in iodine which may explain its reputation as a useful treatment for goitre. Its high level of potassium could similarly explain a reputation for guarding against high blood pressure. In fact, Kombu is reputed to be the answer to an enormous variety of bodily complaints. Again, I can't vouch for its curative properties, but I do know it adds depth and flavour to any savoury dish. Add it to cooking beans to help soften them and impart extra nutrients. Either rinse and dry the Kombu strip for re-use (up to three times) or shred it and add it to soups, stews and bakes. It can be roasted in the oven then ground for use as a flavouring compound, or try deep frying pieces as an unusual alternative to potato crisps.

Nori or laver or laverbread as it is called, is a rich source of vitamins A, B and C, and calcium and protein. It has a mild flavour and is often served with fried foods as it aids digestion and helps the body break down cholesterol. Laver is cooked sea vegetable, usually sold in tins, and occasionally fresh in markets in Wales and Ireland. It is generally used in a sauce flavoured with orange, or mixed with oats and shaped into little cakes to be fried for breakfast. Add it to soups or try it as a pâté with melba toast for an elegant starter. Nori is Japanese laver that has been cooked, dried and cut into fine sheets about 8 inch (20cm) square. Nori sheets are the Japanese equivalent of sliced bread for sandwich making. All manner of items can be wrapped in nori from vinegared rice to Feta cheese. In the same way as other sea vegetables, it can also be added to soups, stews and bakes to give added flavour, or ground fine and sprinkled over food as flavouring.

Tofu

Also known as bean curd and occasionally soya bean cheese. First the beans are cooked and ground to make 'milk', then salts, which act like rennet in cheese making, are added to separate the bean 'milk' into curds and whey. The set curds are what we buy as tofu. Although the process of tofu making is, in some respects, quite like cheese making, the tofu curds are not aged or ripened like cheese. Tofu is extremely rich in protein and calcium and low in calories. It is easily digested (unlike beans!), which, taken together, make it an ideal food for invalids, children and women who are keen to keep up a high calcium intake. Like sea vegetables, it is a real 'health' food and deserves a more important place in our diet. It has a bland flavour that appeals to babies but not adults, so it must be well seasoned if it is to gain any credibility with most eaters.

Silken tofu is a soft, smooth variety most suited to creamy sauces, dips, soups and ice-cream. It is the vegan equivalent of cream or yoghurt.

Smoked tofu is ideal for chopping and adding to pies and casseroles or simply slicing and frying. Because of its lovely smokey flavour, it is perhaps the best introduction to tofu.

Firm tofu is inexpensive and infinitely useful, it

becomes more firm when boiled or if it has been frozen. Introduce flavours by marinading with just about anything from Piccalilli to miso to tomato purée, or add it plain to well flavoured soups or stews.

Mushroom and Dabberlocks Pasty

Dabberlocks comes from the west coast of Scotland and, like all sea vegetables, it is rich in essential minerals and vitamins. It has a gentle flavour which makes it a good introduction for those unused to sea vegetables. Sour cream pastry is splendidly crumbly, but if you prefer a less rich crust, use the pastry recipe in the Baking chapter on page 44. If you can't get dabberlocks, use arame instead.

Pastry:

8 oz (225g) flour
3 oz (85g) butter
5 oz (140g) sour cream

Filling:

2 onions
8 oz (225g) mushrooms
1 tablespoon (15ml) oil
6 oz (170g) red lentils
⅓ oz (10g) packet dabberlocks
2 teaspoons (10ml) dried tarragon
1 tablespoon (15ml) soy sauce

To make the sour cream pastry, rub the flour and fat together until it looks like fine breadcrumbs, then mix in the sour cream. If it seems dry, add about 1 tablespoon (15ml) of cold water depending on the flour used. Work the pastry into a ball, wrap, and allow to rest in the fridge for at least 30 minutes.

It is always wise to check sea vegetables to ensure they don't contain any small shells or stones. Fry the finely chopped onions and mushrooms in oil for 2–3 minutes. Add the lentils, dabberlocks, tarragon and soy sauce to the pan together with ¾ pint (425ml) of water and simmer, tightly covered, until the mixture is fairly dry and the lentils are soft (about 30 minutes). Allow the mixture to cool.

Roll the pastry into an oblong about 15 inches x 12 inches (38cm x 30cm) and lay the filling along its length. Roll up the pastry to form a neat oblong, enclosing the filling. Roll the pasty onto a greased baking sheet, the join should be underneath, and brush the top with egg or water. A generous sprinkling of poppy or sesame seeds would make an attractive finish.

Bake the pasty in a moderately hot oven 375°F/190°C (gas mark 5) for 25–30 minutes. Serve hot with mashed turnip and sprouts or whatever your favourite vegetable may be, or cold with salad. Mushroom and Dabberlocks Pasty travels well and is excellent for lunch boxes and picnics, making a pleasant change from the more usual quiches.

Vegans could prepare the pastry with *Tomor* or oil.

Vegetable and Smoked Tofu Bake

A simple layered bake of grated vegetables and smoked tofu. Serve it with baked tomatoes and your favourite green vegetables for a hearty meal on a cold day. Any combination of root vegetables can be used—you don't need to stick to the ones I've given. Why not try parsnips, Jerusalem artichokes or turnip?

8 oz (225g) smoked tofu
1 lb (455g) carrots
½ lb (225g) onions
1 lb potatoes
3 tablespoons (45ml) soy sauce
2 tablespoons (30ml) oil

Grate the smoked tofu, as you would grate a piece of cheese. Peel and grate the carrots and onions into two separate heaps. Grate the washed potatoes, making a third heap. Oil a casserole or soufflé dish with one tablespoon (15ml) of oil. Starting and finishing with potatoes, fill it with alternative layers of vegetables and tofu. Drizzle the top with the remaining oil and one tablespoon (15ml) of soy sauce.

Cover the dish with foil and bake in a moderately hot oven 375°F/190°C (gas mark 5) for one hour. Remove the foil and bake for a further 20–30 minutes until the top is crisp and golden. Leftovers make a handy addition to your next stir fry or soup-stew.

Tofu and Arame Soup-Stew

Soup-stews and stir fry meals probably constitute the main style of eating for most vegetarians of long standing. We have learned to move away from the main item and two veg notion of a meal, and a quick soup-stew followed by fresh fruit and fromage frais seems a lot less hassle than grinding nuts and toasting breadcrumbs at the end of a day's work. The fact has to be faced that most people have neither the time nor the inclination for fancy cooking, and this is where soup-stews come in. Served with a chunk of bread—garlic if there's time, pitta of plain wholemeal bread if there isn't—they are endlessly variable, healthy, wholesome meals in themselves. One of the questions I am most often asked is 'What do you really eat?'. The simple answer is something like the following recipe most of the time.

2 onions
3 sticks celery
½ heart of a small cabbage
3 carrots
2 large potatoes
1 teaspoon (5ml) dried thyme
pinch chilli powder
2 tablespoon (30ml) oil
3 oz (85g) red lentils
2 tablespoons (30ml) tomato purée
½ oz (15g) arame
2 tablespoons (30ml) miso
juice of ½ lemon
8 oz (225g) firm tofu

Chop the vegetables into bite size chunks and put them in a large saucepan with the mixed herbs, chilli powder and oil and fry for 2 minutes. Add the lentils, tomato purée and dry, crushed arame and 2½ pints (1½ litres) water. Bring to the boil and simmer uncovered for 20–25 minutes until the vegetables are cooked and the lentils are soft.

Add the drained tofu, cut into bite size chunks, and simmer for another minute to warm the tofu. Sir in the miso and season with lemon juice. If you want more of a thick soup rather than a vegetable stew, scoop out about half of the vegetables (before adding the tofu), liquidize them, and return the purée to the rest of the ingredients to re-heat for a few seconds. Serve the soup-stew in big bowls with chunks of bread.

Coriander and Nori Crispies

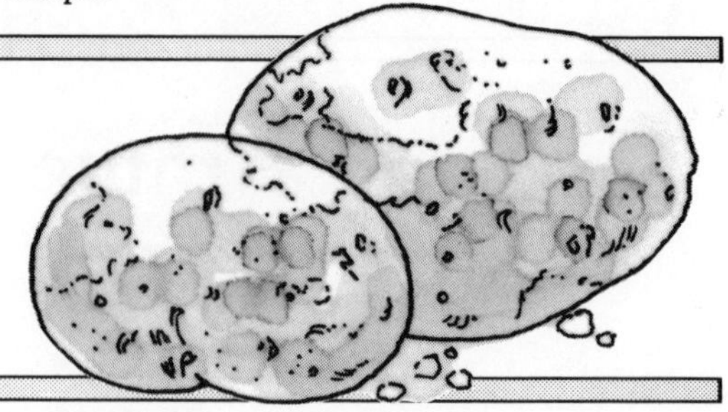

This recipe can't fail to be a hit! It may contain yet another variety of sea vegetable and a batter based on unfamiliar gram flour, but it is so delicious that even the most virulently anti new foods freak will love them. Try them with an elegant salad as the introduction to a smart meal or pile them on baked beans for the kids. Nori is delicately flavoured, traditionally used to wrap dainty Japanese sushi rolls. It also helps the body break down cholesterol, useful for vegetarians who eat a lot of dairy produce.

2 sheets nori
¾ lb (340g) mashed potato
3 tablespoons (45ml) finely chopped fresh coriander—or chives or parsley
juice ½ lemon
1 teaspoon (5ml) soy sauce
vegetable oil for deep frying

Batter:
4 oz (115g) gram flour
scant ¼ pint (140ml) cold water

First, toast the nori. Hold a sheet about 4 inches (10cm) above a full gas jet or hotplate and move it slowly over the heat. You will see the nori darken and crisp as it toasts. When you have toasted the nori, scrunch it up in your hands and sprinkle it, in small bits, over the mashed potato. Add the chopped herbs, lemon juice and soy sauce and mix well together. Now the mixture must be rolled into balls, using clean, wet hands. Use a generous teaspoonful (5ml) if the crispies are for a smart meal, otherwise a good tablespoon (15ml). The balls freeze well, and I often stock up the freezer, ready to provide the basis for an instant meal another day.

When all the balls are ready, prepare a batter by whisking the gram flour and water together. Don't worry about lumps, they will magically disappear. Dip each potato ball in batter and deep fry until crisp and golden. Serve with wedges of fresh lemon.

Pan Fried Tofu for Two

This dish only takes a few minutes to cook but preparation must begin at least a couple of hours ahead to allow the tofu to soak up flavours. Serve it with creamy mashed or crisply roasted potatoes and vegetables such as sprouts, carrots and parsnips, or on a bed of brown rice with a stir fry of beanshoots, peppers, celery and sweetcorn, spiced with ginger and soy sauce. Tofu is a much maligned food. It is quick and easy to use, stunningly versatile, virtually fat free, highly nutritious and deserving of a more important place in every cook's repertoire.

8 oz (225g) firm tofu
1 large onion
2 tablespoons (30ml) Dijon or coarse-ground mild mustard
2 tablespoons (30ml) soy sauce
1 tablespoon oil
¾ pint (425ml) water
1 teaspoon (5ml) cornflour

The tofu must first be pressed to remove some of its liquid and make space for it to take up the flavours in the marinade. If you are really in a hurry, half an hour will do for marinading, but a few hours is to be preferred. Wrap the tofu in 5 or 6 sheets of kitchen paper and squeeze it gently. Repeat the process, but this time sit a weight of some kind (such as a bag of sugar, in a plastic bag to keep it dry) on top.

Peel the onion and cut it into 4 thick rings. Unwrap the tofu and slice through its middle to make two portions. Spread both sides of each piece with mustard. Don't worry about the quantity as mustard loses its pungency when heated, so the finished dish will be gently flavoursome. Put 2 onion rings on a plate and sit one mustard coated, tofu slab on each ring. Top each piece of tofu with an onion ring. Don't refrigerate them, just leave on one side for as long as possible to take up the flavours.

Remove the onion rings, chop them finely, and fry in a tablespoon (15ml) of oil, until quite brown. Push them to one side of the pan and add the tofu pieces and their marinade. Fry for 2–3 minutes on each side. Remove the tofu from the pan onto warm plates and add the water and cornflour (first creamed with a little of the measured water) to the pan, together with one tablespoon (15ml) of soy sauce. Boil rapidly, stirring continuously for a few minutes until the sauce is rich and thick. Serve poured over the tofu and your chosen vegetables. The gravy could be seasoned with 1 tablespoon (15ml) of miso instead of soy sauce.

Baked Avocado with Buckwheat and Smoked Tofu

This makes a substantial starter for a special meal, or serve a bowl of soup followed by the baked avocado and a salad for a mid-week treat. Smoked tofu couldn't be easier to prepare and its strong flavour and firm texture make it an ideal introduction to this calcium and protein rich food. Remember that the avocado must be warmed, not cooked, or it will become unpleasantly bitter. The filling is also excellent in a pie shell, or try it cold for a summer salad meal with a fan of ripe avocado slices and a simple tomato and basil salad. One of the pleasures of vegetarian cookery is the sheer versatility of so many recipes, this one being a case in point!

2 large ripe avocados

Filling:
1 onion
1 green pepper
1 tablespoon (15ml) oil
6 oz (170g) smoked tofu
3 oz (85g) buckwheat grains
2 tablespoons (30ml) redcurrant or gooseberry jelly
2 tablespoons (30ml) soy sauce
¼ pint (140ml) water

Finely chop the onion and pepper and fry until cooked, but with a little crunch remaining. Chop the tofu into tiny cubes and add it to the cooked onion and peppers. Put the buckwheat in a small saucepan and roast the grains over a gentle heat until they smell richly nutty and have taken on a good brown colour. This takes about 4–5 minutes. Add the redcurrant or gooseberry jelly, two tablespoons (30ml) of soy sauce and the water. Bring to the boil, then cover tightly and simmer for 10 minutes. The grains should not be stirred, or like rice they will become sticky.

At the end of 10 minutes check the grains. If they are soft, fine; if not, you may need to add a tablespoon (15ml) of water and give them another 5 minutes. The cooked grains should be soft and almost dry. Stir the grains into the chopped tofu mixture.

Ten minutes before you want to serve this dish, set the oven to 400°F/200°C (gas mark 6). Halve the avocados and remove their stones. Pile each half generously with the filling, lay them in a dish and heat in the oven just long enough to heat the filling and gently warm the avocado. I like them with chips—well, we all have our little weaknesses!

Spinach and Kombu Savoury

Kombu imparts valuable minerals, especially calcium, potassium and iodine when added to beans as they cook and is also rich in a substance called algicinic acid, which binds up toxins, helping the body cleanse itself of poisons. Kombu also softens beans, helping to stop them splitting: how often have you seen the look of red beans ruined by exploded skins? Try a kombu strip next time. This quick and easy dish is excellent with a jacket potato and steamed carrots.

1½ lb (680g) frozen spinach
6 oz (170g) green or 'continental' lentils
4 strips kombu
3 tablespoons (45ml) soy sauce
12 oz (340g) cottage cheese

Begin by draining the spinach. Either thaw it for a few hours in a sieve so that most of the water drains away and the rest can be squeezed out, or put it in a saucepan over a gentle heat until the liquid flows, then boil it fiercely until it is quite dry. Cover the lentils with ½ pint (285ml) water, add the soy sauce and kombu strips and simmer for 20–25 minutes until the lentils are soft (continental lentils don't need soaking).

Remove the kombu from the pan, allow it to cool then shred it finely and return to the lentils. Mix the lentils into the drained spinach and pile it into a lightly oiled dish. Top with a layer of cottage cheese. Bake the savoury in a hot oven 425°F/220°C (gas mark 7) for 10 minutes to heat through.

You can elaborate on the basic dish by adding a chopped red pepper and some sweetcorn kernels to the cottage cheese and topping the whole with a layer of breadcrumbs mixed with Parmesan or Geska and a few mixed herbs for a tasty, crunchy topping. Or try a layer of well-browned, fried onions, followed by a layer of sliced tomatoes before topping with plain cottage cheese. Or you could miss out the cottage cheese altogether and opt for a layer of mashed potato instead. The variations are endless.

Vegans could use crumbled firm tofu, seasoned with a little soy sauce or a few herbs, instead of cottage cheese.

Carragheen Chocolate Mousse

This is a sweet way of using carragheen or Irish moss, another variety of sea vegetable. There has been some controversy about carragheen being carcinogenic, but this refers to chemically treated and processed carragheen: this recipe uses carragheen in its natural form. Dress up the chocolate mousse with whipped cream and chopped hazelnuts for a dinner party or serve it plain for more everyday occasions. Carragheen tends to contain sandy grit and even, sometimes, tiny shells, but this won't present a problem if you are careful. It is quite bulky and hardly weighs anything at all. Don't be put off by wondering how to weigh such a small quantity. It is all an inexact science anyway, so your best guess will be perfectly good enough.

½ oz (15g) carragheen
1½ pints (850ml) milk
1 stick cinnamon
7 oz (200g) plain chocolate
2-3 tablespoons (30-45ml) Grand Marnier or Brandy—optional

Begin by soaking the carragheen in a large bowl of cold water for 15 minutes. The moss will expand wonderfully and float to the top of the water and any grit will collect at the bottom of the bowl. Scoop the moss lightly from the bowl leaving any grit undisturbed in the bottom. Place it in a saucepan with the milk and cinnamon and simmer very gently for 15 minutes. Don't throw away the soaking water, but give it to your plants. About one third of the valuable minerals will have leached into the water making it a nutritious feed for the plants—a pity to pour it down the sink!

Break the chocolate (use a good quality bitter one if the mousse is for a special treat) into small pieces and melt in a bowl over a pan of simmering water. When the carragheen is cooked, pour it through a sieve into a mixing bowl. Use the back of a spoon to push most of the moss and a little of the cinnamon into the mixing bowl. It is important to get as much sieved moss into the bowl as possible because this is what sets the mousse.

Whisk the melted chocolate and alcohol, if you are using any, into the milky moss mixture. Pour it into 6 little chocolate pots, or whatever, to set. If the mousse is for a party, a thick layer of créme fraîche topped with a layer of toasted, crushed, hazelnuts and a pinch of cinnamon would be nice. Whoever would have guessed that seaweed could taste like this?!

Substitute bean milk and carob for a vegan mousse.

Strawberry Fantasy

This recipe uses agar, another sea vegetable, to set a fruity yogurt jelly. I prefer to use agar flakes than chemically treated agar powder, but it is a matter of what is available in your area. The jelly will be firmer than one made using gelatine, a product made from boiled bones, cartilage and tendons—not something the average vegetarian is happy about eating. This jelly is very pretty with its swirls of red strawberry juice and white yogurt. Once you have the basic idea there is nothing to stop you inventing all sorts of different combinations. Let me know your favourites.

½ pint (285ml) water
5 tablespoons (75ml) agar flakes
8 oz (225g) thick yogurt
8 oz (225g) strawberries—fresh or frozen
juice ½ lemon
3 teaspoons (15ml) honey

Measure the water into a small saucepan and sprinkle on the agar flakes. Bring the water to the boil and simmer gently for 3–4 minutes until the flakes are dissolved and the water looks clear. If you are using agar powder, mix 2 generous teaspoons (10ml) to a paste with a little cold water taken from the measured ½ pint (285ml) before adding it to the pan. It has a tendency to become lumpy without this initial creaming. Liquidize the strawberries with the lemon juice and honey. You need ½ pint (285ml) of fruit juice, so, depending on your fruit, you may need to add a little water to make it up to the required amount.

Pour two thirds of the dissolved agar into the strawberry juice and one third into the yogurt, and beat each separate mixture to thoroughly incorporate the agar. Have to hand a 1½ pint (850ml) bowl. Rinse the bowl with cold water first to help the jelly unmould later. Pour alternate quantities of the two jellies into the bowl to give a swirly effect and leave the jelly for an hour or two to set, before serving with extra fresh fruit.

Swap the yogurt and honey for silken tofu sweetened with maple syrup to make a vegan Strawberry Fantasy.

6. Exotic Fruits and Vegetables

This chapter gives only a hint of the glories of the fruits and vegetables now available from the most mundane of fruiterers, let alone exotic ethnic shops. Fast and sophisticated transportation, holidays abroad, our immigrant populations who import their native foodstuffs and the eternal quest for something new have combined to give us our current wealth of choice.

But it isn't only the folk of the 1980s who go gastronomic globe trotting. Eliza Acton wrote over 130 years ago of 'cocoa-nut soup' and fresh limes as if they weren't especially unusual. However, she felt it necessary to say of the tomato, which she called tomata and clearly regarded as exotic, that 'with a clear conscience, we can say we like them in every way they have ever been fixed for the palate'. If you care to go even further back, you can trace the English taste for items such as pomegranates, rose water and spices to the Arabs, better known as the dread Saracen adversaries of the crusading Christian knights. The disagreement was purely religious — both sides were obviously agreed on good food, as medieval English cookery demonstrates.

Examples of new foods coming in from all parts of the world and influencing our cookery are legion. I believe this ability to accept, appreciate and assimilate new ingredients is one of the strengths of English cookery. Now, thanks to atmosphere controlled containers and air freight, we have the produce of the entire world at our fingertips. In centuries to come, who can say with certainty that the passion fruit of the West Indies will not be as much a part of Christmas food as the Arabian pomegranate, introduced so long ago and now an absolute necessity for the overflowing bowl of nuts and fruits at my mother's traditional Christmas table in the north-east of England.

Do bear in mind what I say earlier in the book about the quality of food being of paramount importance. This especially applies to tropical fruits and vegetables. Where possible, buy organically grown produce — by which I mean produce grown without any artificial fertilizer or chemical pesticides, insecticides, fungicides or herbicides. Don't be bamboozled by fine words on packages. If produce labels say something like 'grown entirely without artifical chemicals' then it's organic and worth the price. If the label is not entirely clear, it is usually for the very sound financial reason that someone wants to make 'organic' profits without following laborious and expensive organic growing codes. When in doubt, ask. And if you are not happy with the reply, don't waste your money paying the price that genuine organic produce quite reasonably commands. As a well known television character from London's East End might say: 'When in doubt, leave it out!' Where profits are concerned there aren't many people one can trust. The Soil Association is an exception. They award their symbol, a sort of curvey triangular shape, only after very rigorous checks. Other trustworthy producers of honestly organic produce you may come across are Demeter, Nature et Progrés, Bio Top, Fresa and Suolo e Salut.

There is a nasty system whereby manufacturers of unpleasant agricultural chemicals which are banned or severely restricted in the West simply export them to developing countries. This immoral and unpleasant little wheeze for keeping up company dividends is known as the Circle of Poison or Pesticide Triangle. Countries like our own export them, developing countries use them, and we then import the crops grown with these toxic substances. Residues of chemicals are a worrying problem in **all** foods, both home grown and imported. According to the Association of Public Analysts in 1986, only £1 was spent on checking our food for safety for every £10,000 spent on groceries. That same year, in a report published on pesticide residues by the Ministry of Agriculture, Fisheries and Food, one sample of fruits and vegetables was found to be 20 times above accepted international limits. I recommend buying organic whenever possible!

Setting aside concerns for the quality of our food, let's consider another aspect of exotic produce. There's a wealth of exciting new developments being coaxed along by farmers in warmer climes, soon, perhaps, to take their place in our ever widening culinary repertoire. Cookery writers may find themselves offering recipes for Pejibaye palm fruits, said to be a chestnut-like fruit with a near perfect combination of protein, fat, carbohydrate, vitamins and minerals for humans. Or perhaps you prefer the sound of Nunas beans, which apparently cook something like popcorn. There's also the cocoyam, the leafy quinoa and the scarlet flowered amaranth. The trendier food stores in America are already offering protein-rich amaranth flour, cookies, breakfast cereals and even bread. I can't wait for it to arrive here! I wonder if it will become as familiar as the kiwi fruit?

A Sampling of Exotics

Ackee

A fruit, which like the familiar tomato, is treated as a vegetable. The ackee, *Blighia sapida*, is named after Captain Bligh, who introduced it to the West Indies. It came originally from West Africa, but it is now so plentiful in the Caribbean that it is sometimes called 'free food'. The fruit of an evergreen, it has a shell which hardens as it ripens, splitting open when fully ripe to reveal three large black seeds, surrounded by yellowy white, fleshy arils. This is the edible part — the seeds are poisonous. Ackees are only available in Britain in tins, to be found in Indian as well as Caribbean shops. They are a vegetable version of scrambled eggs!

Artichoke (Globe)

A member of the thistle family, it is thought to have been introduced into Britain during the reign of Henry VIII. They are available from May till September, but at their best during July and August. Choose firm, heavy globes with no dry edges. The leaves should have a slight bloom. Avoid any that have fuzzy or discoloured centres. Leaves cut during preparation for cooking should be dipped in lemon juice to stop them browning. When all the leaves are removed you will see the choke, which must be cut out or pulled away. The best part of the artichoke is the heart, which lies immediately below the choke.

Artichoke (Jerusalem)

No relation to the globe artichoke. It is a tuber of the sunflower tribe and was introduced to Britain in the early 1600s. The plants look like huge, towering sunflowers minus the flower. 'Jerusalem' is thought to be a corruption of the Italian *girasole*, which means 'following the sun' — nothing to do with the Jerusalem of the Holy Land despite those recipes with names like 'Palestine' Soup. Jerusalem artichokes are available from October to February. The knobbly tubers should be free from too much dirt. Avoid small, slug eaten, bruised or broken specimens.

Aubergine

Also known as eggplant, eggfruit and even, sometimes, guinea squash, they were introduced here from Asia in 1597. They are available all year round. The skin is usually glossy purply black, but green, white and yellow varieties are available. Choose plump, firm, glossy fruits without bruises or brown patches. I don't believe it is necessary to salt them to reduce the bitter juices. In my experience, modern aubergines are no longer bitter. Grilled, fried or baked they are delicious, but boiling reduces them to a rather unpleasant tasting mush. Dishes containing aubergine are almost always best cooked the day before required and left for the flavours to mature and blend, rather like the best of curries.

Avocado

Used by the Aztecs and Incas as both food and beauty aid. They are available all year round. They come smooth skinned, like the Ettinger and Nabal, slightly rough like the Fuerte, or with a very knobbly skin like the Hass, which has the best flavour in my opinion. Cradle the avocado in your palm to test for ripeness. It it gives under gentle pressure it is ready. To hasten ripening of hard fruits, put them in an airing cupboard, or with a ripe apple in a paper bag. To avoid the fruit going brown when peeled, rub it with lemon juice. Should you be a devotee of old cookery books, you will sometimes find avocados called 'alligator pears' . . . the Fuerte, perhaps?

Breadfruit

The awful Captain Bligh brought back seedlings of breadfruit from Tahiti for the British planters in Jamaica. It originated in Indonesia and New Guinea and is one of the staple foods of the South Pacific. It is available throughout the year, especially in stores selling West Indian foods. It is a large round vegetable with a rather knobbly, pale greenish-brown skin, hard and white inside. Fry it in thickish slices or boil it like potato. It also makes splendid crisps. Boiled or steamed breadfruit mashed with plenty of milk and butter or coconut milk is delicious — though it is more dense than potato so a little goes a long way! It can also be baked slowly, like a jacket potato. Leftovers make a good fry-up. It has a disconcerting way of getting cold remarkably quickly, so serve it without delay.

Opposite A Mushroom Parcel with Garlic Cream (page 60) and Water Melon Sorbet (page 62).

Carambola
Also sometimes called star fruit. They are grown in China, India, South-East Asia and South America. They're generally available around Christmas, but as supplies increase, so will availability. The carambola is a five-sided, yellowish green fruit, about four inches (10cm) long. It has a delicate, slightly sweet-sour flavour, perfect for enliving the breakfast muesli. Or try it in a fruit salad, or serve it lightly poached with ice cream or custard. The star shaped slices (you don't peel them) are a visually amusing addition to almost anything. Choose firm fruits with a good waxy sheen. The more yellow they are, the better their flavour.

Cassava
Also called manioc, this is a fleshy tuber, originally from Brazil but now grown throughout tropical countries. It is a starchy vegetable, used in the same way as a potato. It can be peeled, cubed, boiled and mashed, or baked in the oven.

Christophene
Also called chocho, chow chow, chayote or vegetable pear, because that is rather what it looks like. It originated in Mexico but supplies mostly come from the Caribbean and West Africa. There are many varieties, but our supermarkets and West Indian stores usually only stock a smooth skinned, pale green one. They are marrow-like in flavour, though the flesh is somewhat firmer than that of a marrow, and should be treated in much the same way. They are said to be very good for reducing high blood-pressure.

Coconut
A nutritious staple of the Caribbean. Not only is it rich in protein, oil and vitamins A and B, it's also an economically important crop because its outer fibre makes excellent floor coverings and its oil superb suntan lotion. Coconuts are available all year in Britain. Choose one that is heavy in your hand and, when you shake it, makes a splashing sound. The shell should be quite dry, especially around the 'eyes'. To open a coconut, pierce two of the three 'eyes' (a knitting needle is the perfect tool) and drain the liquid. Technically, this isn't coconut milk; you prepare that by processing the white flesh with water in a blender, then sieving the mixture to get milk, which will keep in the fridge for up to two weeks. Meanwhile, back with our nut, having drained the liquid, stand it on its 'eyes' and hit it with a hammer to expose the creamy flesh. Freshly grated coconut will keep in the freezer for up to six months.

Opposite A Gourmet Meal in a Hurry (page 74-9).

Colocassi, Dasheen and Eddoes
These are all members of the colocasia family. Colocassi, large and rough skinned, are widely used in Greek cookery. Dasheens are elongated tubers with brownish, hairy skin. Eddoes are much smaller, rounded tubers with the same brownish, hairy skin. All are potato-like foods to be peeled and boiled, fried, baked or roasted, though dasheen has a slightly bitter flavour which is best removed by boiling.

Custard Apple
They grow in the West Indies and South America. There are many varieties but the most common in this country is a smooth skinned variety of the annona species. There is another called the cherimoya, which has a rough skin quite like a pine cone. Eat them raw by simply slicing and scooping out the fragrant, creamy white flesh which tastes like a delicious cross between banana and pineapple.

Gourds

I'm using this term to cover a wide variety of vegetables, including dudi and karella, and even custard squash and pumpkin. They are all from the marrow family and are treated accordingly, i.e. boiled, baked, stuffed or made into chutneys and jams. Karellas, or bitter gourds, are especially popular in Asian households. The bitterness can be reduced by soaking in water for an hour before cooking. Gourds and squashes come in just about every shape and size you can imagine. Some are even kept and dried as ornaments because they look so attractive. Hollowed-out small gourds make splendid containers for vegetable salads. Bottle gourds, which (surprise, surprise) look like bottles, were once used as containers for gunpowder, so if you feel their marrow flavour is a bit average for cooking, they have plenty of other uses! And I'm sure you don't need reminding that pumpkins not only make great pies, they make horrifying, candle-lit faces for Hallowe'en as well.

Guava

Brought to Europe by the Spaniards after their conquering exploits in South America. The skin is thin but tough, starting off green and becoming more yellow as the fruit ripens. Guavas are particularly rich in vitamin C, so try them next time you feel a cold coming on. They have a powerful, musky scent when fully ripe. Cup the fruit gently in your hand — if it gives slightly, it is ripe. Try them just sliced and scoop up the delicate pinkish white flesh with a spoon. The seeds and skin make an excellent base for jam or cheese (as in lemon cheese/curd). Try them poached in syrup or serve them sliced with a little mound of cream cheese as well as in fruit salads.

Kohlrabi

A hybrid of the cabbage family, it is sometimes called the knol kohl or turnip cabbage. It came to Britain around 1580 but has only recently resurfaced. It is available throughout autumn and winter and is much used in Greek cuisine. Kohlrabi can be white, pale green or purple and has a pleasantly light, turnipy, nutty flavour. Buy small, tender young roots without worm holes, avoiding any that are wizened or discoloured. The leaves can be cooked as spinach and anything that you do with turnip can be done with kohlrabi. They are especially good grated raw, tossed in a good mustardy dressing and served as a salad — perhaps in a colourful gourd shell?

Kumquat

Miniature oranges with a thin edible rind. Their name comes from the Cantonese 'kam kwat' meaning gold orange, and indeed they originate from China. They look stunning however you use them, especially if you can also get a few leaves for decoration. The whole fruit can be eaten fresh, though I find them quite sharp. Try them poached in syrup and added to ice cream or to top a chilled sweet soufflé. Or decorate a rich fruit cake with them instead of the more conventional nuts and cherries. They can be candied to make a pretty accompaniment to after-dinner coffee, as well as pickled, preserved in brandy or made into jam.

Lychee

Another Chinese fruit. Small, with a thin, brown, rough, scaly shell, which peels away easily from the soft, almost jelly-like, white flesh. Available from November to March, they now grow in many countries including Madagascar, Mauritius and Israel. They are excellent raw, but they can be poached in syrup or added to savoury dishes for their sweet-sour flavour. A Chinese emperor once sent hundreds of miles (mule train only in those days!) to have supplies rushed to the capital for his favourite concubine. Perhaps we should adopt them as a St Valentine's Day treat in view of this romantic tale — they're a lot less fattening than chocolates!

Mango

There are 35,000 varieties of mango. It is acclaimed as the most delicious of exotic fruits, its history going back over 6,000 years. Available all year round, they come in an enormous range of shapes and colours. Buy firm, unblemished fruit and ripen them in a warm place at home. They are at their delicious best when fully ripe and soft to the touch. Lay the mango flat side down on a chopping board. With a very sharp knife, slice off one side, as close to the large flat oval stone as possible. Turn the fruit over and repeat your slicing. You should now have two good pieces of fruit and a wonderful stone for you or the children to munch the rest of the fruit from — messily but happily!

Mangosteen

Despite its name, the mangosteen is not related to the mango, and despite the colour of its flesh it is not related to the lychee either. The mangosteen comes from South East Asia and is the fruit of an extremely slow growing tree. It tastes something like a ripe greengage and looks vaguely like a reddish-brown, leathery skinned apple. The skin cuts away to reveal five segments, each with a seed. The fruit is very pretty to look at when served whole with the top half of its skin cut away to reveal the flesh. It has a delicate flavour and is best eaten fresh on its own or in a fruit salad, though it can be used to make a delicately-flavoured sorbet.

Mooli

The mooli is an enormous, mildly-flavoured, long white radish. The ancient Greeks offered radishes fashioned in gold to Apollo at his temple in Delphi, and the slaves of ancient Egypt kept body and soul together with a staple diet of onions and radishes. I can only say I hope they had something more flavoursome than the mooli! Use it freshly grated or sliced in salads or add it, cut into slivers, to a stir fry. It can be carved into amazing shapes — with compensates, perhaps, for its lack of flavour.

Okra

Also known as ladies' fingers because of its dainty shape, this vegetable came to America with the slaves from Africa. It became a firm favourite in the Deep South and is an important element in 'gumbo', a rich soup stew, popular in both the West Indies and America. Okra is also much used in Indian cookery. The small tapering pods contain a mucilaginous (gluey) juice which gives gumbo its character. If you want to extract the juice before cooking with okra, soak the sliced fingers for an hour or two in a bowl of water to which you have added a good dash of vinegar. Choose okra that are small, crisp and slightly under-ripe. They can also be eaten raw in salads; their shape, vaguely reminiscent of the carambola, makes a pretty garnish.

Passion Fruit

The passion fruit has a wonderful scent and flavour. About the size of a plum when fully ripe, it has a purplish-brown, wrinkled skin — it is not ready for eating if the skin is smooth. It is a classic addition to Pavlova, but it can be turned into a jam-like preserve or made into ices and sorbets. Or the seeds can be sieved out and the juice added to cocktails and fruit punches. The simplest way to eat passion fruit is just to scoop the juicy seeds up with a spoon.

Paw Paw
A native of America, but now grown in most tropical countries. They are available all year round. This large pear-shaped fruit is amazingly versatile. The under-ripe ones can be stuffed and baked as a main course. The lusciously ripe ones can be eaten rather like melon, with a squeeze of lemon or lime juice or a little crystallized ginger. It has a green-yellow, quite unattractive skin, becoming more yellow as it ripens. The centre contains peppery black seeds which I have known used as a spice, but which are generally discarded. You can give your hands and neck a tenderizing beauty by rubbing them with freshly peeled paw paw skin and leaving for 30 minutes before rinsing off with lashings of cold water. The softening you will notice is due to papain, a tenderizing agent in the fruit. The carnivores amongst you can use this virtue to tenderize tough meat!

Plantain
Looking like giant bananas, they are only eaten cooked. The plantain is a staple in West Indian and African diets. They can be green and underripe, or yellow and ripe. The more yellow they are, the sweeter they'll be. To peel them, chop off the top and bottom, then score along the edges through to the flesh. Slice into manageable-sized pieces, then lay them in a bowl, cover with boiling water and leave to soak for 10 minutes. You will find the skin peels away quite easily. They can be boiled or fried once peeled, or baked in their skins (but don't forget to make a few cuts to avoid them exploding). Ripe plantains are very good cooked in their skins over a barbecue. Don't confuse plantain with green bananas. Green bananas are exactly that — small (ish), green, unripe bananas. They too are a starchy potato substitute to boil and mash, but they don't taste as good as plantain in my view.

Quince
This doesn't really belong in a list of exotics because it isn't grown in tropical climes. I've included it here because it is *regarded* as exotic by modern cooks. It is a delicious, if ugly, member of the pear family. An emblem of love and happiness in times long past, quince are either round or pear-shaped with a yellow, fluff-covered skin and a wonderful aroma. The white flesh turns pink when cooked. They are available from autumn into early spring. They are a brilliant addition to any apple pie and make wonderful jam and jelly. In fact, quince jam, 'marmello' in Portuguese, is the forerunner of marmalade. They were once a much used item in British cookery and it really is time we revived them, so I hope you will give me licence to mention them here, even if a little out of place.

Rambutan
From the same family as the lychee, it is sometimes known as the hairy lychee. It looks a bit like a little furry animal, with its soft hairy covering of dark brown spines. Make a small cut in the skin then peel it away to reveal the soft white flesh inside. Treat them in much the same way as lychees. The stone in the middle isn't edible.

Sweet Potato
First brought to Europe in the late 1400s they became known as the Spanish potato, for Spain is where they were mostly grown. They should not be confused with yam, which I will deal with further on. They have a chestnut flavour and fairly dry, mealy fresh. Their skin can be pale cream or brownish red. They should be boiled or baked whole in their skins to retain all their delicately sweet flavour. They make a wonderful change from the more usual baked spud. They also make great crisps.

Tamarillo

From the same family as tomatoes, they're sometimes called tree tomatoes, Java plums or Jambolans. They are imported from New Zealand and Kenya. The egg-shaped fruit has a tough skin which peels away easily from the stalk end if the fruit is first put in hot water for a minute or so. The tamarillo is very rich in vitamin C. Serve it peeled and sprinkled with sugar or honey, or poached or grilled with savoury dishes. In fact this is exactly how the tomato used to be treated — it wasn't always only a savoury item! Tamarillo, like tomatoes, make excellent jams and sweet preserves as well as providing a good base for ice cream.

Yam

Although similar to the sweet potato, the yam is not so sweet. It has a brownish pink, rough skin with white flesh. They can grown to enormous sizes — up to 100 feet (30m) long. There are many different varieties, some with splendid names like haffoo, ranta and pumpum. They are available all the year round and are most often found in West Indian or Asian stores where they may be called Indian potato. Again, yam is used, and tastes, much like potato. Try adding a little cinnamon, orange peel, nutmeg and a tablespoon or two of apple purée, when you've boiled and mashed them, for a really different 'potato' dish. Yams also go well in any vegetable stew.

Exotic Lime Pie

Limes may look like mean little green tinged lemons, that you feel tempted to leave on the shelf — but I hope you won't! Fresh limes have the most stunningly delicious flavour imaginable. It's not unlike that of the lemon, but more subtle, slightly sweeter and rather less tongue shrivelling. They are rich in vitamin C and were once a compulsory part of every British sailor's shipboard diet. They cure scurvy, so our healthy sailors were in a good position to create the British reputation for mastery of the high seas. That's why, to this day, the word 'limey' is still used to name the British. If you can't get limes, lemons are a perfectly acceptable substitute. Should you eat fish or meat, I'd recommend you to try lime rather than lemon in your next dish. Choose bright green, heavy, glossy fruits. Once they start turning yellow, they lose that lovely sharpness that makes them so delicious.

Your favourite pastry recipe prepared with 6 oz (170g) flour

4 limes
¼ pint (140ml) milk
2 eggs
4 oz (115g) sugar*

Line four individual pie tins (4½ inches, 11cm in diameter) with very thinly rolled pastry. Reserve a little pastry for lids which are to be added later. You can prepare one large pie if your prefer. Use metal tins if possible — they heat up quickly once in the oven to give a crisp, well-cooked base to the pies. China and glass may look prettier, but they will inevitably make your pastry soggy!

Take three of the limes and scrub them thoroughly with warm soapy water to remove preservatives on the skin and at least some of the pesticides that may have been sprayed on them. Put them, whole, into a small pan and cover with cold water. Bring them to the boil, put a lid on the pan and simmer for 15 minutes. Pour off the water and allow the limes to cool for a minute or two. In the meantime, put the milk, eggs and sugar into your liquidizer, together with the juice of the fourth lime. I use white sugar, it's cheap and gives a pleasant, light light result. If you refer the flavour of brown sugar, there is no reason why you shouldn't use it. Just remember that it is not any better for you than white! — see the section on sugar in the Children's chapter.

When the limes have cooled a little, chop them roughly, removing any seeds, and add them to the ingredients in the liquidizer. Process until you have a smooth, rich cream. Pour the cream into the pastry-lined tins and cover the mixture with a lid of thinly-rolled pastry. Make sure you seal the edges well. Cut a couple of holes in the top of each pie to let the steam escape, brush with milk or water and sprinkle liberally with sugar. Bake in a hot oven, 425°F/220°C (gas mark 6), for 30 minutes. Serve the pies hot or cold with lashings of cream or sweetened yogurt.

* This recipe gives 4 oz (115 g) sugar, which makes a deliciously sharp tart. If you have a sweet tooth, increase the sugar to 6 oz (170g).

Cheese and Onion Chocho

2 chochos (christophenes, chayotes, chow chows or vegetable pears)
2 medium-sized onions
8 oz (225g) fully-matured Cheddar cheese
4 oz (115g) fresh wholemeal breadcrumbs
2 tablespoons French mustard

You will find this Caribbean vegetable fruit under many names, but the most common is probably christophene. It looks a bit like a large, pale green, ridged pear. Its texture and flavour lies somewhere between marrow, courgette and cucumber. It is an easy, adaptable, new addition to the culinary repertoire and well worth trying. I have been a little mischievous in choosing this recipe, which may be the first one you have come across for using chocho. Here we have a thoroughly exotic item paired with the most mundane of English ingredients, yet it's a typically Caribbean combination. The flavour is often described as 'subtle' or 'bland'; however, I would describe it as a fresh, green flavour that is gentle but definite. It can be boiled and mashed, covered with breadcrumbs and flashed under a grill for a different vegetable side dish. Or boil one whole, split it in half, scoop out the centre and fill with a peppery sauce of raw onions, garlic, chilli and vinegar. Add a little tofu — smoked or plain — to the sauce and you'll have a splendid main course. Bake one filled with crumbled macaroons and mincemeat and you'll have a very different pudding.

Slice the chochos in half along their length, in the same way as if you were preparing an avocado. Use a teaspoon to scrape out most of the chocho (save the flesh and the small, heart-shaped seed!) to leave you with neat, empty shells. Chop the scooped out flesh and seed quite finely and place in a bowl. Peel and grate the onions and add them to the bowl together with the grated Cheddar, fresh, soft breadcrumbs and mild mustard. Mix the whole lot well together and pile it into the chocho shells, packing it fairly firmly. Place the stuffed halves into a casserole dish and put just enough water into the dish to barely cover the bottom. Cover with a lid or foil and bake in a moderate oven 350°F/180°C (gas mark 4) for 1 hour. Serve this substantial dish hot with mushrooms and broccoli in winter, or cold with a good salad in summer. Somehow the chocho retains a splendid crispness — this is where the cucumber qualities come in — despite the fact that it is perfectly well cooked.

Vegans may like to try this dish with a little Marmite or miso, and two or three tablespoons of tomato purée instead of cheese. You will also need to add an extra ounce or two of breadcrumbs, a handful of peanuts, or some sunflower seeds, sesame seeds or pine nuts to make up for the bulk (and protein) of the cheese. You'll find it tastes as good as the cheese version!

Okra with Coconut Cream and Cashews

Okra, a plant of the marrow family, has a variety of names, of which ladies' fingers is perhaps best known; it is also called gumbo in the Near East, bamia in France and bhindi in India — so take your pick. It is vitally important to choose small, green, crisply fresh pods. There is nothing worse than tough, over-sized stringy old okra! Okra features as a main ingredient in gumbos, rich soup-stews which usually contain poultry, seafood and/or sweetcorn in a supporting role. These dishes have come to epitomize the food of America's Deep South, imported by the slaves who were uprooted from Africa and the Caribbean to work on the plantations. This recipe is Latin American in style with a hint of India from the spices. Serve this creamy vegetable dish on a bed of rice, with bread (anything from pitta to French stick) or with cous-cous or bulgur for a substantial main course. I'm particularly fond of both bulgur and couscous because they are light to eat and so quick to prepare. Leftovers re-heat or make an excellent salad base. I'd urge you to try them both soon, if you haven't already.

¾ lb (340g) okra
2 small green chillies
2 tablespoons oil
2 or 3 cloves garlic
1 teaspoon ground cumin
1 tablespoon ground coriander
6 oz (170g) onions
1 oz (30g) coconut cream
3 oz (85g) peanuts
3 oz (85g) broken cashews
4 or 5 tablespoons finely chopped fresh coriander leaves if available

Rinse the okra and slice off the stalks, without cutting into the green finger itself. De-seed and chop the chillies, not forgetting to keep your hands well away from your eyes when preparing them — and don't lick your fingers either! (Wash your hands well when you finish handling raw chillies.) Heat the oil in a good-sized pan, then add the chillies, as much crushed or chopped garlic as suits your taste, the cumin and the ground coriander and fry gently for a minute or two, then add the peeled and roughly chopped onions. Continue to fry for two or three more minutes. Add the okra to the pan together with a pint (570ml) of water and the coconut cream. Bring to the boil, then simmer for 10 minutes or so. Meanwhile, toast the peanuts in a small frying pan over a gentle heat until they're golden brown. You may want to oil or butter the pan lightly, but it isn't absolutely necessary. When the peanuts are toasted, grind them smooth and add them to the stew. If it is very thick, add an extra ¼ pint of water. Toast the cashews in the same way as the peanuts, then add them directly to the stew. Just before serving, add the finely chopped, fresh coriander leaves to the mixture. Serve piping hot.

Colocassi in Honeyed Wine

2 lb (900g) colocassi
½–¾ pint (425ml) rough dry wine (white or red)
4 or 5 cloves garlic (or however much or little you like)
2 tablespoons runny honey
4 tablespoons oil — preferably olive oil
8 oz (225g) onions
1 medium cauliflower

Colocassi can be used whenever you would use potatoes. This recipe is from Famagusta, where, unusually, it is often cooked without meat. In the rest of Cyprus and Greece you will find it a common ingredient in pork or chicken dishes (if you eat such things), and sometimes in thick vegetable soups. In true Cypriot style, this recipe should be begun at least a couple of hours before you want to serve it, to allow time for the vegetable to marinate in the wine. Apart from allowing the initial marinading time, the recipe couldn't be simpler. Serve the stew as a main course, in large soup plates, liberally topped with thick Greek yogurt. It goes without saying that it should be 'Greek warm', not steaming hot! Feel free to add a handful of olives, some capers or a bunch of chopped coriander to vary the flavours. I am sure the hospitable inhabitants of Famagusta wouldn't mind you making adjustment to their dish — and I have to admit I prefer it with a liberal dose of every one of my suggested extras. For good measure, I usually stir the yogurt directly into the pot before serving to make a splendidly creamy sauce — but I assure you it is quite delicious the way the black clad women of Famagusta traditionally serve it!

Peel the colocassi, slice into chip-sized little logs and pile them into a casserole. Mix together the wine, crushed garlic and honey, and pour over the colocassi. Stir everything thoroughly, cover and leave it to marinate for at least two hours. Heat the oil in a large pan and lightly brown the peeled and chopped onions. Add the colocassi, together with the marinade, to the onions. Bring to the boil, cover and simmer for 30 minutes. Add the cauliflower, which should be chopped into bite-size florets, and continue to cook for a further 5–10 minutes until the cauliflower is tender. Allow the mixture to cool a little before serving. If you are bored with onions use celery instead, and for a change from cauliflower you could try carrots, leeks, broccoli or broad beans — in fact, this is a totally flexible dish and will accommodate itself to whatever you have in. If you intend to add a pot of thick Greek yogurt, remember it should be added after the pan has been taken off the heat or it will curdle.

Cassava Biscuits

1 lb (455g) cassava root
1 small coconut, which should yield 8 oz (225g) grated coconut
4 oz (115g) muscovado sugar
4 oz (115g) plain flour
3 oz (85g) butter or vegan margarine
1 teaspoon baking powder

Cassava is available throughout the year in West Indian shops. It will keep for two or three weeks in the bottom of the fridge, provided you don't cut into it. I can't think of a better way of introducing cassava to your household than these biscuits, which are crisp on top and moist inside. The cassava is grated and the juice squeezed out to leave a dry meal. The meal is for the biscuits, and the juice will be used in Jamaican Pepperpot Soup later in this chapter. You'll see I've used brown sugar in this recipe. Its flavour adds authentically Caribbean style to the biscuits. As for the freshly-grated coconut — well, I'm not sure the effort involved in draining, cracking, peeling and grinding to get a bowl of moist, pure white flesh is worth it! A bag from the supermarket seemed very desirable the day I dealt with four fresh coconuts one after the other, each with a shaggy beard that had to be cut away before I could even see the 'eyes', let alone pierce them. Perhaps I'm jaundiced, so I'll leave it to you. If you prefer the easy option of a supermarket pack, make sure it has no added sugar or you'll upset the proportions in the recipe.

Peel and grate the cassava. You can either use an ordinary grater (which isn't too difficult) or process it in a food processor till it is quite fine. Put the meal in a cloth, or better still a jelly bag, and squeeze it firmly to extract as much juice as possible — reserve the juice for the Pepperpot Stew. Drain the coconut, smash the shell with a good blow from a hammer and extract the flesh. Slice away the tough brown skin and rinse the coconut. Process it, like the cassava, until it is fine. Alternatively, you can grate it by hand, but this is quite an effort.

And now you've done all the hard work, the rest is simplicity itself! Put the cassava meal and grated coconut into a bowl, add the sugar, flour (white or wholemeal as you prefer), chopped butter or vegetable margarine and baking powder. Rub the fat into the other ingredients. You will have quite a moist and sticky mixture. Pile it into a greased tin about 8 or 9 inches (20–22cm) square. Pat it down and smooth over the top. The cassava mixture should be ½ inch (1cm) deep. Use a fork to make the surface thoroughly rough and coconut textured. Bake in a fairly hot oven, 400°F/200°C (gas mark 6), for 30 or 35 minutes until brown and crispy on top. Slice into fingers and serve hot or cold. The biscuits go equally well with a dish of fresh tropical fruits or a cup of coffee. Keep them in a tin as they tend to dry out quickly.

Liza's Ginger and Coconut Hillocks

Fresh (green) ginger is increasingly seen in supermarkets that stock exotic produce, but I have an idea it is rarely used in anything but savoury dishes. Most people are used to the idea of ginger in curries and we are all used to crystallized ginger. Liza's little sweets combine sharp, fresh ginger with the richness of freshly grated coconut, a combination that is well known in the Caribbean but not in England. They are very sweet, but as an occasional treat they shouldn't do too much harm to the waistline and can be positively beneficial if you are off colour. Ginger will help relax and calm an upset stomach and alleviate the discomfort of gastritis or period pains. It has even been found to help in cases of travel sickness. A fresh ginger root will keep for some weeks in the fridge. If your root starts to put out shoots, why not plant it? It will grow quite happily in a pot on the windowsill and makes a pretty plant. Once peeled, the root will keep for months if covered with sherry or salted water. There really is no substitute for the flavour of fresh ginger; dried ginger has far less pungency. Again, the problem with this recipe is preparing the coconut flesh, but once that has been done they are very easy to make. Somehow ready-grated coconut just doesn't have the same flavour so the effort is worthwhile.

1 small coconut
4 oz (115g) ginger root
½ pint (285ml) water
12 oz (340g) sugar

Drain the liquid from the coconut, smash the shell and extract the flesh. Cut away the thin brown skin, rinse and put in a food processor. Peel the ginger and add it to the coconut. Process them together until they are finely chopped. They will look remarkably like chopped hard-boiled eggs. Put the water and sugar (brown or white as you prefer) in a pan and bring it to the boil. Add the grated coconut and ginger and bring it back to the boil. Keep your eye on it as it will do its best to bubble over and make a nasty mess all over your hob! Boil the mixture for 20–30 minutes until it is reduced to a thick sticky mass. Butter or oil a sheet of greaseproof paper while you give the coconut and ginger mixture a minute or two to cool. Use two teaspoons to shape little hummocks of the mixture to be left to set on the greased paper. Entirely simple and quite delicious. They will keep for weeks.

Kolokotes

Kolokotes are another typically Cypriot dish. They are pasties (or one big pie if you don't care for tradition) filled with pumpkin. They are usually eaten on cold winter days for breakfast, when the Greek Orthodox inhabitants of Cyprus are avoiding meat and eggs before a religious service. However, it has to be said that kolokotes for breakfast, or any other meal, don't represent a hardship. They are easy to prepare (though you must begin at least 12 hours ahead), ideal for packed lunches or picnics and have a most unusual and agreeable flavour.

I think the recipe must be very old because it contains a typically medieval combination of ingredients, and the crossing of the boundaries between what is savoury and what is sweet serves to confirm this. Sweet tarts of spinach and savoury pies with currants and sugar were the norm around the fourteenth and fifteeth centuries, but while sweet spinach tart doesn't appeal to twentieth century palates, I'm sure kolokotes will. If you can get sweet Cyprus pumpkin, obviously that's best, but any pumpkin will do.

Eat the pasties on their own or serve them hot, with a green vegetable and gravy for dinner. If you want to be really daring you could also try them with custard! We clearly have much still to learn from the vegetarians of the past.

1 lb (455g) pumpkin
3 oz (85g) raisins
2 oz (55g) cracked wheat (bulgur or pourgouri)
2 teaspoons cinnamon
½ teaspoon ground cloves
2 tablespoons oil — preferably olive, but corn will do
2 tablespoons water
generous grinding of black pepper

wholemeal pastry prepared with 12 oz (340g) flour
(if you are making only a pie lid you will need far less pastry)

Peel the pumpkin, discard any seeds or stringy bits, and chop the flesh into small cubes. Place in a bowl with all the other filling ingredients. Stir the mixture well and leave it in the fridge overnight. The raisins will swell and the cracked wheat will soften a little. If you can leave it for 24 hours, so much the better, but 12 hours will do if you're in a hurry.

Prepare the pastry and divide it into portions. Roll each into a circle, give it a generous few spoonfuls of filling, moisten the edges with cold water, fold it into a pasty shape and seal the edges well. Go round with the tines of a fork to ensure you have a really good seal as well as a pretty edging. The number of pasties you make will depend on how big you want to make them. Lots of small ones for the kids' lunch boxes or fewer, bigger ones for bigger appetites? If you don't have the time to shape pasties but would like to try the mixture anyway, you could pile it into a casserole to be topped with a pastry or potato lid. Pasties take 20–25 minutes in a fairly hot oven, 400°F/200°C (gas mark 6). A pie will need 45 minutes at the same temperature. Your taste buds will be astonished and delighted by your culinary daring.

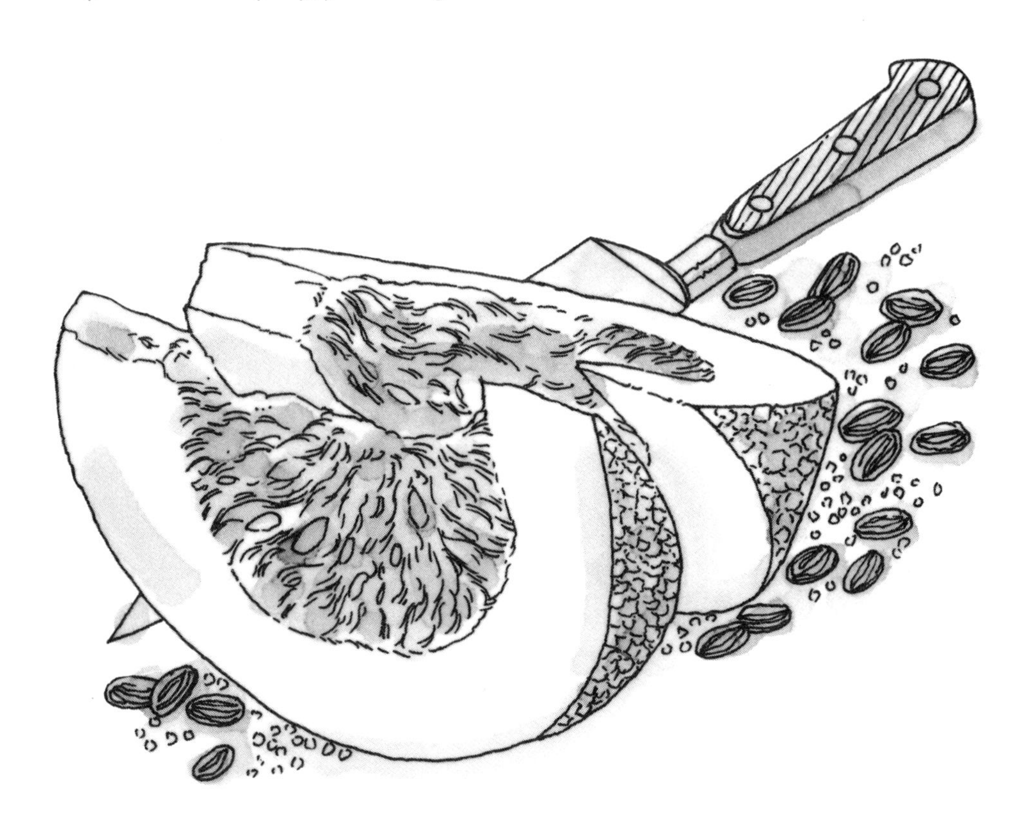

Priscilla's Pumpkin Pie

This wonderfully gooey pie is from America's New England. Pumpkin pie is an indispensable part of the Thanksgiving for that first American harvest. The Founding Fathers were introduced to pumpkin — or, rather, squash — by the native Indians, the word squash being derived from an American Indian word. Pumpkin was commonly grown in Britain, according to Tusser's Five Hundred Points of Good Husbandry *(1573), and by the seventeeth century, Apple and Pumpkin Pie was highly regarded by both rich and poor, its popularity only waning with the industrial revolution — I suppose no one had time for cooking! Most American recipes are quite sweet so I've modified this one to suit our less sugar addicted palates. A dash of brandy or sweet sherry, or even a couple of ounces of rum-soaked raisins added to the mixture before baking, would not be out of place in this celebratory pie.*

Having prepared the pumpkin purée, you will have a good number of discarded seeds. Why not keep them? Preserve them, Greek-style, for chewing in idle moments; it really is very simple. Wash the seeds, removing any clinging stringy bits, and dry them in a tea towel. Spread them on a baking sheet and give them a generous sprinkling of salt. Bake them in a moderate oven for 20 minutes. You should eat only the kernel, scattering the empty shells like a peasant gently passing the time—you'll have to use your imagination for the shady olive grove! Incidentally, pasatempo *is the Greek name (borrowed from Italian) for these roasted pumpkin seeds—it literally means passing the time.*

Orange Pastry:
6 oz (170g) wholemeal flour
3 oz (85g) butter
1 orange

Pumpkin pie filling:
1 lb (455g) pumpkin flesh, peeled and chopped
2 tablespoons molasses
2 oz (55g) muscovado sugar
2 eggs
½ pint (285ml) milk
1 teaspoon cinnamon
½ teaspoon ground nutmeg
½ teaspoon ground ginger
¼ teaspoon ground cloves

Prepare the pastry by rubbing the fat into the flour. Wash the orange and finely grate the rind, which should be rubbed into the fat and flour. Squeeze the juice from the orange. Two tablespoons should be about right to bind the pastry together. Cover the pastry and allow it to rest for 10 minutes or so while you prepare the filling.

Put the pumpkin into a pan with barely enough water to cover the base of the pan. Bring to the boil, cover and simmer for 15–20 minutes. Keep your eye on the pan and only add a tiny amount of extra water if it seems absolutely necessary. You want the pumpkin soft and as dry as possible. Hopefully you won't have any water to pour away before mashing the pumpkin smooth. Set it to one side to cool a little while you roll out the pastry and line a greased 9 inch (22cm) flan ring — you already know by now that metal is best. Add the rest of the pie filling ingredients to the pumpkin purée and beat the mixture smooth. I know it's a bit disappointing to see the bright orange of the pumpkin take on a muddy tone from the molasses, but I promise the flavour is worth it. If you really insist on an orange pie, use white sugar instead of the two brown ones given in the ingredients. Bake the pie for 10 minutes in a fairly hot oven 425°F/220°C (gas mark 7), then turn the temperature down to 400°F/200°C (gas mark 6) for a further 25 minutes.

If you want to dress the pie up for a special occasion, a piped border of stiffly beaten double cream will do the job nicely. Or you could decorate the top with halved pecans (much more authentically American than walnuts) and rum-soaked raisins. Without added cream this is a surprisingly healthy pie with quite a low sugar content, despite its luxuriously rich, mouth-watering texture.

Paw Paw Baked with Walnuts

Paw paws can be unripe, i.e. hard (which is what is required for this recipe), or as ripe and soft as a perfect melon. Slices of ripe vibrantly orange-red peeled paw paw alternated with pale Honeydew or Galia melon look stunning. You could arrange paw paw slices in a fan with sliced avocado dressed with walnut oil or vinaigrette, and serve them with dainty fingers of brown bread and butter. The meat eaters amongst you may like to try a slice of prosciutto wrapped round paw paw as a stylish change from melon—friends tell me it is an excellent combination. Vegetarians can try the same idea using smoked tofu or Haloumi cheese. And ripe paw paw with preserved stem ginger is altogether more exciting than plain melon and ginger. So there you are, a host of ideas.

Paw paw is also useful as a treatment for rough skin that could do with a little loving attention. Follow the directions in the first section of this chapter and your hands, elbows, knees, neck or whatever, will feel as soft and cherished as if you had spent the afternoon in an expensive beauty clinic.

Opposite Tofu and Arame Soup Stew (page 87).

2 paw paws
¾ lb (340g) onions, peeled and chopped
1 tablespoon oil
1 teaspoon mixed herbs
2 cloves garlic
4 oz (115g) walnuts
1½ oz (45g) fully matured Cheddar cheese
1 × 15 oz (425g) tin tomatoes

Slice the paw paws along their length, and scoop out the black seeds from the centre. Fry the onions in the oil with the mixed herbs and as much or little garlic as you like. After a minute or two, add the walnuts and fry for two more minutes. Tip the contents of the fry pan into a food processor, add the cheese, and process the filling until it is quite finely chopped, but not a paste. Drain the tomatoes, reserving the juice, and finely chop the tomato flesh, adding the seeds to the reserved juice. Stir the chopped tomato into the filling. Give each paw paw a generous topping of walnut filling and lay the halves in casserole. Pour enough tomato juice into the bottom of the dish; any leftovers can go into soup or stock. Baker the covered dish in a fairly hot oven, 400°F/200°C (gas mark 6), for 1–1½ hours, until the paw paws are thoroughly tender. Serve hot or cold.

Ackee Islands

2 ripe plantains
2 tablespoons oil
1 red pepper
good pinch ground nutmeg
pinch sugar
pinch chilli powder
4 thin slices bread
1 tin ackees—they only come in one large size
4 tablespoons chopped fresh parsley

This recipe makes a stunning dish, either as a starter or as one of many courses in a grand meal. It is simple to prepare, and if your guests haven't come across ackees before, they will think you've given them the best scrambled eggs they've ever eaten. Ackees can only be bought in tins, but don't let that put you off. Many Indian grocers stock them as well as Afro-Caribbean shops. Vegetarians can try them cold, dressed with vinaigrette, or hot, mixed with fried onions and chick peas. In this recipe, the ackees are mixed with red peppers, served on crisply fried bread, encircled with fried plantain and topped with a generous sprinkling of parsley — a colour combinations that would please anyone from the West Indies.

Choose quite ripe plantains. more yellow than green—they'll taste much sweeter. Don't be misled into buying green bananas. Plantain is much, much bigger than banana. So, if it isn't huge, it isn't plantain. The plantain makes a delicious partner to ackees and really gives you the flavour of the Caribbean. If you want to serve this as a main course, a suitable side vegetable would be spinach or callaloo, which is a spinach-like vegetable, but I think it is substantial enough to be served alone. If it is to be a starter, make the portions small as it is quite filling.

Opposite Baked Avocado with Buckwheat and Smoked Tofu (page 90) and Carragheen Chocolate Mousse (page 92).

First peel your plantains, which may look like bananas but they don't peel in the same way. Chop off the top and bottom, then score along the sides. You want plantain strips as long as possible, so find a shallow dish that you can lay the plantain flat in, then cover them with boiling water. Once they've soaked for two or three minutes they will peel perfectly easily.

Each plantain makes two servings. Slice them lengthways and trim a little off the rounded sides to make four good slices. Fry the slices in hot oil on both sides and keep warm. In the meantime, slice the pepper into fine matchsticks and fry them, with the nutmeg, sugar and chilli powder, in a little oil until soft. Cut the sliced bread into four circles that will fit the plantain strips when joined at the ends to form a circle. Fry the bread until crisp. Stir half the drained ackees (use the rest some other way or use them all for very large portions) into the fried pepper and heat through. Lay a circle of bread on each of four warm plates. Surround each with a little 'wall' of fried plantain, secured with half a cocktail stick. Fill each one with the pepper and ackee mixture, topping them with a generous dusting of parsley. If your guests aren't used to Caribbean foods, they will be instantly converted!

Jamaican Pepperpot Soup

This soup is actually a combination of two Caribbean specialities, Pepperpot Soup from Jamaica, and Pepperpot Stew from Trinidad and Guyana. They both contain meat, so I can't claim this is an entirely authentic recipe, though my ingredients (except for one, which I'll explain in the recipe itself) are entirely in keeping with this most traditional of dishes. The main difference between the two dishes is cassareep: the stew should have it but not necessarily the soup. Cassareep is made from the juice of cassava, so if you've tried the Cassava Biscuits earlier in this section, you'll have some cassava juice to hand. West Indian shops sell bottled cassareep, which is a commercially prepared, thick dark sauce made with sugar, salt, cinnamon and cloves. The squeezed cassava juice left over from the biscuits contains a fair amount of starch and it is this which acts as a thickener. As cassareep may be difficult to obtain, I'm using the basic ingredients but not the actual bottled sauce. Cassava, rather like paw paw, seems to have meat tenderizing properties. I've noticed my hands always feel much softer whenver I've handled cassava. I wonder if you will notice a difference too?

Pepperpot stews, so the stories go, can last for years, with new ingredients being tossed into the pot whenever needed, the whole lot preserved by the spices and cassareep — believe it if you like! I can't claim my soup will last for generations, but I can confidently say it is a meal in itself. I've also included a recipe for Corn Meal Dumplings to add to the soup, making it even more substantial.

Jamaican Pepperpot Soup:
1 tablespoon oil
3 cloves garlic
1 tablespoon dried thyme
2 or 3 green chilli peppers
1 stick cinnamon
6 whole cloves
1 medium-sized sweet potato
8 oz (225g) pumpkin
15 oz (425g) tin tomatoes
2 oz (55g) coconut cream
3 pints (1.7 litres) water
8 oz (225g) cooked red kidney beans
juice squeezed from 1 lb (455g) cassava — roughly ¼ pint (140ml)
1 bunch large spring onions — a speciality of West Indian shops
6 oz (170g) large leaf spinach
4 tablespoons miso

Corn Meal Dumplings:
4 oz (115g) coarse corn meal
4 oz (115g) wholemeal flour
1½ teaspoons baking powder
good pinch nutmeg
good pinch cinnamon
pinch salt
1 tablespoon oil
just enough water to bind

Begin the soup by heating the oil in a large pan. Add the crushed garlic, thyme, de-seeded and chopped chillies, cinnamon stick and the cloves tied in a piece of muslin for easy retrieval later. Have ready the peeled and chopped sweet potato and pumpkin. They should be in quite small dice. Add them to the pan together with the tomatoes, coconut cream and water. Bring it all to the boil and simmer for 25 minutes.

While it cooks, make the Corn Meal Dumplings. Mix the dry ingredients, add the oil and just enough water to make a soft dough. I don't normally use salt, but these dumplings do taste better for just a pinch. (They're good with any soup or stew.)

Now add the cooked kidney beans, the cassava juice, the chopped onions and the finely shredded spinach, to the soup, Shape the dumpling dough into tablespoon-sized balls and drop them into the simmering soup or a separate pan of boiling water. The dumplings and green vegetables will be cooked after 6 or 7 minutes. Scoop the dumplings into warm, large, soup plates. Mix the miso with just enough cold water to make a smooth paste and add it to the soup in the pan. Stir it well, then ladle it over the dumplings.

Of course, you've guessed it, miso isn't exactly Jamaican. But it does add a lot to the flavour when you can't get cassareep!

7. Cooking with Herbs and Flowers

Recipes which make the best use of herbs and flowers are invariably old, a direct link with kitchens long gone. The history of cooking and eating is fascinating. Food is intrinsic to every aspect of life, from Jewish chicken soup that lovingly cures everything to dry bread and water as punishment for anything. Food reflects our history, both in fact and folklore, as well as marking high holy days and personal joys or sorrows. In England, we have a wealth of regional cookery which has, sadly, been largely ignored. Many of the dishes we eat at particular times, like the Shrovetide pancakes in this chapter, have a long and venerable history. The ingredients used in old recipes often have charming and, in some cases, practical folklore woven around them. The cowslip, most English of flowers, was used in the same way as borage flowers in the ancient recipe given in this chapter. The tiny crimson drops in the cowslip's chalice were said to be fairy favours capable of restoring youthful bloom, and indeed they have long been used as a tonic for the heart. On a rainy day, when the little folk are safely tucked inside the cowslip, you may perchance hear the soft, sweet singing of fairyland voices.

To put it all in context, here is a brief cook's tour of our culinary heritage. The conquering Romans were noted for their love of good food. They planted plums, quince and mulberries, orchards of apples and pears, and vines, of course, to supply their gourmet needs. Despite what I regard as an unhealthy interest in eating dormice, they fully appreciated a wide range of vegetables—unlike their medieval successors. When they left, so did their influence. The plantings remained, but little trace of ancient Rome has survived in modern English cookery.

The monks of the Middle Ages may have been a source of light in dark times, and though they skilfully grew medicinal herbs, the food of the time was hardly gourmet. Banquets were exceptions: they could be of breathtaking splendour. From this time springs the rhyme about four and twenty blackbirds baked in a pie, singing to please the king when the crust was opened. It probably happened just as the song says. The pie would have been a grand 'conceit' for some sumptuous occasion. A master cook would have shaped a pie, or coffin as it was called, baked it, then carefully inserted the live birds through a hole in the base. Such conceits were an important part of banquets for centuries, designed to show the skill of the cook, the status of the host and the importance of the guest.

With the Tudors came both confidence in world affairs and an upsurge of all that was delicious for the table. From this period come some of the most delightful recipes for using flowers in cookery. The food in our taverns was the envy of Europe, and the English had a reputation as the best fed nation on earth. The Puritans changed all that. In the mid-seventeenth century mince pies were declared nothing more than 'flat idolatry', much was banned from the kitchen repertoire as 'Popish', and England embarked upon a period of pickled herring and plain fare. But looking at the description of Joan Cromwell's salad in my nasturtium seed recipe, perhaps matters weren't so bad—at least for those in charge!

A glance at the recipes favoured by Parson Woodford, a celebrated eighteenth century cleric with gourmet inclinations, shows a continuing culinary excellence. In his diary for May 1789, he bemoaned the lack of gooseberries for sauce to accompany his mackerel (apparently due to a 'very backward' spring that year) — hardly the cry of a man unused to fine food.

In the nineteenth century, food in England took a decided turn for the worse. As the industrial revolution progressed, folk left their villages in droves to work in the newly establishing towns. Good cooking became something of a lost art. For all the empire-building of the Victorians, they failed to attain the culinary exuberance of the Elizabethans. The newly created middle class was riddled with anxieties about what to do, how to do it and when it should be done. They turned to Mrs Beeton, and her directions for household management, as to an oracle. Form, not content, came to be the deciding factor in the kitchen at this time. No matter that the pie was inedible, the tea adulterated or the jelly like indiarubber, that it appeared on the table was all that counted. There were honourable exceptions but, on the whole, good food was rare.

With the Edwardians came some relief, as flavour and style began to regain their rightful position. Between the wars, English food saw a splendid consolidation on the Edwardian foundations. But after the Second World War, we once more lost our way. It took many years and Elizabeth David to retrain the English palate to overcome the legacy of austerity.

Things have now improved tremendously. There is a gentle groundswell of interest in regional cookery, flower cookery is making a comeback and at long last vegetarianism is acquiring a lighter, more flavoursome touch. Changes indeed!

I trust, gentle reader, you will enjoy my selection of herb and flower recipes gathered largely from our past.

Apple Marigold

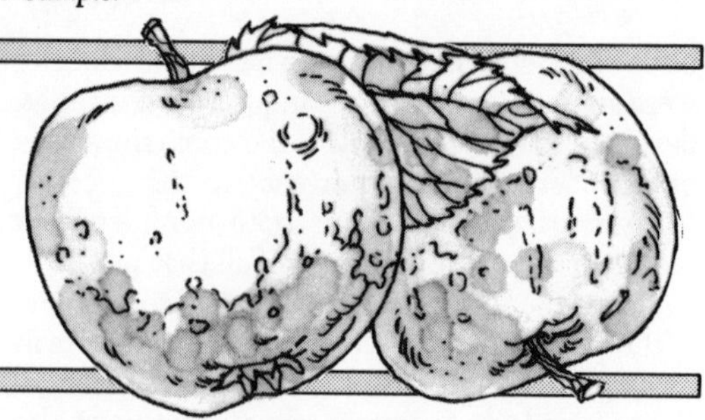

This is an old cottage recipe for a sweet pudding of apples flavoured with marigold petals. Marigolds, by which I mean Calendula officinalis, *otherwise know as pot marigolds, have quite a strong flavour.* Still Glides the Stream, *a book by Flora Thompson which wonderfully evokes a bygone country life, describes some of their uses. The daughter of one of Miss Thompson's characters would laugh and tease her father about his old-fashioned country ideas, pointing out that tastes had changed and people no longer cared for strongly flavoured dishes. Well, I think old Reuben, for that was his name, was right. The old country flavours should never have been lost and it is high time we revived them! Reuben expected his mutton broth to contain a few golden petals and his daughter always made sure he had them, despite her teasing. Pot marigolds were traditionally added to meat stews, as well as being paired with apples, as in this recipe.*

The petals were known as 'poor man's saffron' due to their golden colour. They flavoured cheeses, home baked buns, custard sauces and even gentrified salads in time past. The petals can be used fresh or dried. Choose flower heads that are at their peak. Rinse them only if you must, then pull off the petals. To dry them, simply lay the petals on a tea towel on the central heating boiler or in a warm airing cupboard — sunlight fades them and reduces their potency, as with all herbs. If you want to flavour buns or cakes, soak a few chopped petals in warm milk before using, just as you would saffron. Remember, marigolds are as strongly-flavoured as saffron, so a little will be quite enough.

3 large cooking apples
4 eggs
1 pint (570ml) milk
1 teaspoon marigold petals
2 tablespoons sugar

Peel and core the apples and slice them into rings. Lay the apples in a shallow oven dish. Beat the eggs, milk and marigold petals together and pour over the apples. Sprinkle sugar over the dish and bake in a moderate oven, 180°C/350°F (gas mark 4), for 25-30 minutes. Serve with lashings of cream in the old-fashioned way. If you want to be more health conscious, try thick yogurt or fromage frais instead.

To turn this into a savoury pudding to serve with a jacket potato and perhaps soya or meat sausages, omit the sugar and add a teaspoon of thyme, a teaspoon of sage and lots of freshly ground black pepper to the egg, milk and marigold mixture and bake as directed above. It also goes very well with baked beans and oven chips!

Rose Petal Yogurt

This is a dainty dish for dessert that can be based on thick cream, curd cheese thinned with a little milk, fromage frais or silken tofu, as well as yogurt. The creamy base is flavoured with roses, which were once of supreme importance, looked upon as herbs with a full panoply of healing properties. There are countless old recipes testifying to their past popularity. It was unthinkable that they should be left to wither and die on their stems! In 1550 they were regarded as strengthening for the heart and a cure for shaking and trembling. Henry's VIII's personal version of 'after shave' was a blend of rose oil, rose-water, musk and ambergris. In A Queen's Delight *(1662), there is a recipe for making 'an odiferous perfume for chambers' which consisted of heating together powdered cloves and rose-water, while* Mary Doggett's Book of Receipts *(1682) suggests warming rose leaves with orris root to scent a room. Syrup of roses was regarded as a pick-me-up, and Gerard advocated distilled rose-water to promote sound sleep. Even as recently as the 1920s and 30s Hilda Leyel, an authoritative writer on herbs, offered many recipes for roses, as does a slightly later cookery writer, Constance Spry. Yet now it is rare to encounter a rose recipe. Rose wine, rose ice cream, rose vinegar, rose syrup, rose petal jam, not to mention rose-water and rose pot pourri were once the everyday business of good cooks. What a pity it is no longer so.*

The scented petals dry within a day or two on the central heating boiler or in an airing cupboard. If you intend to eat them, remove the bitter tasting, pale tip or 'heel' before drying. Add dried petals to a bottle of vinegar (cider or white wine is best), and you will soon have something delightfully new to use in salad dressings. Mix the petals with cloves, cinnamon, nutmeg and a handful of dried lavender and fix the scent with equal quantities of salt and orris root for a long lasting pot pourri in the old style. Candied petals are a lovely decoration for cakes or trifles. Follow the instructions given in the Candied Daffodil *recipe for the method. Fresh petals scattered on a salad are a very pretty addition, and who are we to say they aren't health promoting as well as beautiful!*

1½ lb (680g) yogurt
1 oz (30g) toasted slivered almonds
1 teaspoon ground cinnamon
½ teaspoon ground nutmeg
3 tablespoons rose-water
2 tablespoons honey
fresh scented rose petals for decoration

Place the yogurt (or any of the options I give in the introduction) in a fine cloth or jelly bag and hang for 3–4 hours. It will reduce by about one third. Stir in the rest of the ingredients, chill, pile into glass bowls and serve scattered with fresh petals. One of the most delicious ways is to use half fromage frais and half stiffly beaten double cream—but it isn't what you'd call healthy!

Candied Daffodil Posy

This is a stylishly simple, totally modern idea, yet it has its roots firmly in the past when cooking with flowers was a quite the norm. As Wordsworth so aptly put it in his poem 'Daffodils', '. . . my heart with pleasure fills and dances with the daffodils'. And who could resist a dainty daffodil for dessert? 'Jonquille Printanière' was invented about ten years ago by a chef named Ian McAndrew. It has become his trade mark, though many chefs have adopted and adapted his idea. Chef McAndrew's dessert consists of a candied daffodil—yes, they really are very good to eat—sitting on a mound of whipped cream which is covered with sliced kiwi fruit, the whole surrounded by a puddle of red strawberry purée My variation on his theme is to sit the daffodil atop an almond jelly flavoured with rose-water — very fashionable in the eighteenth century. I've chosen to garnish my dessert with young hawthorn leaves. Yes, hawthorn leaves are edible too. Try them in a sandwich next spring! If hawthorn leaves aren't available, sliced orange will be every bit as pretty.

This recipe can be extended to many flowers; pansies, roses, violets, apple blossom, freesias, primroses, lilac, jasmine, even daisies, are all suitable. Should you wish to experiment, use only edible flowers (some are definitely not edible), and use only flowers that you know to be unsprayed with garden chemicals. Sadly, it would be most unwise to rush out to the florist for tonight's dessert, beautiful though it might be! To candy any flower, choose blossoms which have just reached their peak. This is the time when they have the best flavour, though daffodils have a very subtle taste that is virtually overwhelmed by the sugar used for candying. If you want a strong flavour for dessert, you must choose strongly-scented flowers such as roses or violets.

Candied daffodils:
4 daffodils at their peak
1 egg white
1 tablespoon lemon juice
1 tablespoon water
3–4 oz (85–115g) caster sugar

Almond jelly:
1 pint (570ml) milk
1 tablespoon sugar - white gives the better colour
2 teaspoons powdered agar or 4 tablespoons agar flakes
2 oz (55g) ground almonds
1 tablespoon rose water
hawthorn leaves or orange for garnish

To candy the daffodils, cut off the stalks and carefully removed the stamens. Lightly beat the egg white with the lemon juice and water in a good-sized bowl. Run the sugar in a liquidizer until it is extremely fine, virtually powdered. Dip each flower in the egg white mixture, ensuring that it is well coated and that you don't bruise the delicate petals. Next, dip the flower in the sugar. Again, coat it well, but with a delicate touch. Lay the finished flower on a wire rack to dry and harden in a warm place. Store the finished, dried flowers in a tin.

To prepare the jelly, bring a pint of milk, with the sugar, gently to the boil and add the agar. If you use powder, mix it with just a little cold water to a paste or you are likely to end up with lumps! The powder is ready almost as soon as it lands in the milk. If you use the flakes, sprinkle them directly onto the hot milk and stir for 3–4 minutes until they are completely dissolved. Stir in the ground almonds and rose-water and beat the mixture smooth. Pour the jelly into four moulds that you have previously rinsed out with cold water, and leave them to set.

Unmould the jellies onto small plates. Top each one with a daffodil and tuck a few fresh leaves into the base of each jelly just before serving. The leaves can be dipped in egg white and sugar like the daffodils if you have time. Should you want a sauce for this dish, stir a little rose-water into slightly sweetened single cream and surround each jelly with its own miniature cream lake. The jelly also looks very pretty spooned into hollowed out clementines, garnished with candied violets.

Vegans can make almond jelly with soya milk and the difference will be hardly noticeable.

Nasturtium Flower Pancakes

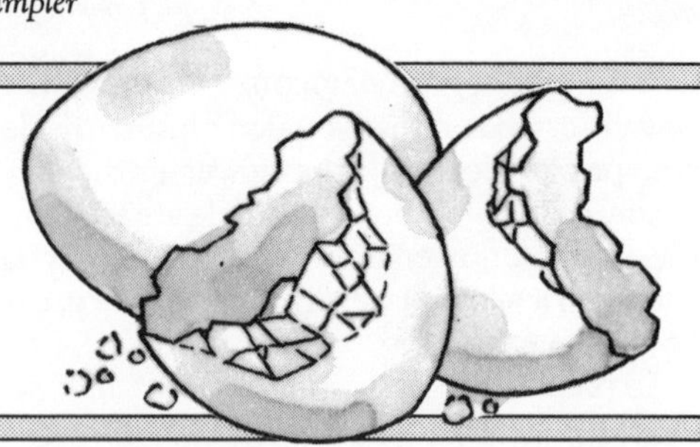

The nasturtium, both seeds and flowers, has been used in English cookery for centuries. Like the pot marigold, it fell into disuse, though I notice my local supermarket is now selling the flowers in little boxes for culinary use, so let us hope the revival continues. Nasturtiums are the easiest of flowers to grow — in fact, you may find yourself struggling to confine them to their allotted space. John Evelyn, in his Acetaria *of 1699, recommends the seeds 'be monthly sown' to ensure a continuous supply from early spring to late autumn if the weather is mild.*

Both flowers and leaves have a sharp, peppery flavour which combines well with cream cheeses or green salad herbs. A most elegant starter can be made from flowers filled with herb or garlic cream cheese, set on a bed of shredded nasturtium leaves — though you have to have nimble fingers, a fair amount of time and preferably a piping bag for the cheese. A splendid vinegar can be made from the flowers by using one of those ready-spiced pickling vinegars that are now available. Boil a pint (a generous half-litre) of vinegar with a few chopped shallots for 10 minutes, then pour it over three or four good handfuls of flowers. Cover, and leave in a cool place for at least three weeks, then strain and bottle it, adding a couple of fresh flowers to each bottle if you have any available. Wouldn't that make a lovely Christmas present or a delicious difference in your next hollandaise? The seeds can be pickled and used as you would capers, but I will deal with them later.

Pancakes are one of the most ancient foods I know of. They can be traced all the way back to the Druidic religious festival of Imbolc, when the Celtic world stretched from Czechoslovakia to Ireland and from Holland in the north to the Po Valley in the south. The Druid's Imbolc became our Shrove Tuesday. So, medieval flowers and Iron Age pancakes—the past flows strongly, even into our twentieth century kitchens!

Pancakes:
5 oz (140g) plain flour
½ teaspoon salt
1 egg
½ pint (285 ml) milk
3–4 tablespoons oil

Filling:
1 lb (455g) cottage cheese
3–4 shredded nasturtium leaves
handful nasturtium flowers
little freshly grated nutmeg

Mix the flour and salt in a basin and whisk in the egg and milk to make a smooth batter. The secret of pancakes is a hot, heavy pan, preferably not too large. The first pancake was at one time put outside as an offering to the garden spirits. This seems to me an excellent and practical idea as the first one is rarely the best. It merely establishes that the batter is thin enough and the pan hot enough. So, oil the pan well, heat it thoroughly and pour only enough batter into the pan to make a thin pancake. Pluck up your courage and toss it—it's really not so difficult—to cook the other side. Continue until have used all the batter. Pancakes freeze well, so prepare a batch in advance if you prefer. To make the filling, mix the ingredients together, reserving a few flowers for decoration. To assemble, simple give each pancake a filling, roll it up and serve garnished with a flower.

Nasturtium leaves contain oxalic acid and should not be eaten in vast quantities, though a dozen leaves or so a week would be entirely safe and healthy. Choose small young leaves, as the largest ones may be too peppery.

Apple Mint Risotto

Risotto is hardly an English cottage recipe, but I couldn't resist this simple dish. At least the mint is typically English! I was given the recipe by a friend who swears it is uniquely his own. He bade me point out that the secrets of a good risotto are first, to stir, stir and stir; and secondly, to use Italian Arborio rice. If you heed his words, you will have a creamy dish that is neither runny nor dry—just what an authentic risotto should be. The mint flavouring, in what is a classic Italian dish, seems to me a stroke of English genius.

There are many varieties of mint, and in my opinion, the best for the kitchen is apple mint. It has rounded, much wrinkled, hairy leaves with a strong scent of ripe apples. The best variety is Bowles' mint, which keeps true to type and fragrance. Its disadvantage is that older leaves change their flavour and are not so pleasant. It also does badly when restricted in a pot, so be resigned to eternal warfare as you attempt to confine it to its part of the garden. Pineapple mint, peppermint and spearmint are other useful and heavily-scented mints worth growing for cooking, as well as pennyroyal. Pennyroyal has a venerable history. The 'royal' derives from its use in great households as a way of ridding royal rooms (and personages?) of fleas. Gerard mentions that it was found at 'Mile End near London', where it was popular with sailors to sweeten their drinking water while at sea, and to get rid of ships' fleas! He recommended it 'to comfort nerves and sinewes' in a refreshing bath. Pliny, centuries earlier, held it to be a most valuable remedy for headache. Peppermint is accepted as a common cure for indigestion as well as being a well-known flavouring for sweets. It is quite a new mint, having only been discovered in 1700. Spearmint, slightly less pungent than peppermint, is an ancient hedgerow plant. It was distilled in water to relieve hiccupping and flatulence, 'a weak stomack and nervous crudities' as John Evelyn put it.

Mint makes a delightfully invigorating pot pourri when dried and mixed in equal quantities with lemon balm. A very old Yorkshire recipe, more or less identical to our modern Eccles cakes, with the addition of a generous quantity of mint and a touch of nutmeg, is also well worth trying. Mint sauce is not the only option!

2 pints (1.2 litres) vegetable stock
1 small onion, peeled and finely chopped
2 tablespoons oil
10 oz (285g) Italian Arborio rice
3 oz (85g) Parmesan cheese
1 large handful chopped, fresh mint leaves—preferably apple mint

Bring the stock to a slow simmer. Gently fry the chopped onion in oil for 2 or 3 minutes. Add the rice to the onion. Stir constantly and ensure it is thoroughly coated with oil. Add ¼ pint (140ml) of hot stock to the rice. Simmer gently and stir until the stock is absorbed. Add another ¼ pint (140ml) of stock, and continue the gentle simmering and stirring until this too is absorbed. Carry on until all the stock is absorbed, stirring tirelessly. It will take about 25 minutes but the effort is worth it! By now you should be about 5 minutes away from a perfectly cooked risotto. If you feel a little more liquid is necessary and you've used all the stock, add a little hot water from the kettle. Don't drown the rice, particularly near the end of cooking. With 5 minutes cooking time left, add the Parmesan (and perhaps a knob of butter if you want) and continue to stir. The rice should be creamy but not runny, tender but *al dente*. Immediately before serving, stir in the chopped mint. Serve with a huge dish of braised mushrooms (truffles would be taking things too far!) and a green salad, and thank Martin for sharing his splendid idea.!

Picked Nasturtium Seed Salad

Old English recipes that mention capers, and many of them do, were often referring to pickled nasturtium seeds. In The Castel of Health *(1539), Sir Thomas Elyot, says 'Capers styreth appetite, being eaten with otimell, before any other meate'. In other words, they encourage a good appetite. They were called 'caphers' by the Elizabethans, who were especially fond of them. A 'grand sallet' described in* The Second Book of Cookery *(1641) gives instructions for a most elegant mixture. The buds of all kinds of good herbs ('herbs' then meant anything green eaten uncooked, such as lettuce, cress and so on), a handful of French capers, seven or eight sliced dates, a handful of 'Raisins of the Sun', a handful each of almonds and currants, five or six figs and preserved sliced orange. These were to be mixed with a little sugar, then piled onto a large dish and decorated with halved lemons stuck with rosemary sprigs and cherries. 'Roasted hart' and boiled eggs were added, and the whole thing painstakingly garnished with more lemons, preserved orange, almonds and capers. If you miss out the meat and sugar, and add a modern salad dressing, it would make a fitting salad for even the most discerning modern vegetarian. Joan Cromwell, wife of the man himself, served a grand salad of equal quantities of almonds, raisins, pickled cucumbers, cooked turnips, shrimps and capers. Substitute smoked tofu for the shrimps, and you have another excellent main course salad.*

In her recipe for pickling nasturtiums, Eliza Acton instructed they 'should be gathered young, and a portion of the buds, when very small, should be mixed with them'. There are many recipes for nasturtium seed 'capers', but I think hers is the best. She simply dissolves 1½ oz (45g) salt in 2 pints (a generous litre) of vinegar and throws in the seeds and tiny buds on a daily basis. Other recipes spice the same quantity of salt and vinegar with a shallot, 6 peppercorns, 3 cloves, a little nutmeg and a sliver of horseradish. Still others also include a chilli pepper, and one I came across adds only a sprig of tarragon and a clove of garlic to the vinegar and salt. Choose which most appeals to your own taste. The pickling pot should be kept covered, in a cool, dark place. The fridge is ideal.

15 oz (425g) tin red kidney beans
1 large avocado
3 oz (85g) black olives—Calamata are the best
3–4 tablespoons pickled nasturtium seeds
1 large green pepper, de-seeded and chopped
2–3 inch (5–8cm) piece mooli or white radish—optional

Dressing:
3 tablespoons oil
1 tablespoon cider vinegar or wine vinegar
½ teaspoon honey

Drain the beans and mix them with the chopped avocado and the rest of the ingredients. I prefer to stone the olives, but it isn't necessary if you are in a hurry. If you do not intend to serve the salad immediately, dip the avocado in a little lemon juice before adding it to the bowl or it will go brown. Mix the dressing ingredients together and pour over the salad, tossing it well. This is one of the quickest, most pleasant salad meals I know for a hot day. Serve it with garlic bread, hot pitta or just chunks of good, fresh wholemeal bread. Follow it with cool melon for a simple, but very satisfying, meal. You can vary the salad endlessly by adding tomatoes, cucumber, celery or raisins and experimenting with butter beans, chick peas or haricot beans instead of kidney beans.

Blackcurrant Leaf Cream

The old country recipes for blackcurrant vinegar (the forerunner, I would have guessed, of modern blackcurrant cordial), dainty blackcurrant leaf sandwiches or this lovely old recipe from Scotland for blackcurrant leaf cream seem quite to have fallen by the wayside.

Blackcurrant vinegar made a sweet, rich sauce for puddings or, diluted with water, soda, champagne or dry white wine, a cooling summer drink. The vinegar is very simple to make and worth trying if you have a currant bush. Pick 1 lb (455g) of currants, bruise them and cover them with 2 pints (just over a litre) of white vinegar; leave them covered, in a cool place, for 24 hours. Strain (take care not to squeeze the currants or the vinegar will be cloudy), discard the blackcurrants (put them in a pie with apples for added flavour?) and pour the darkening vinegar over another, freshly picked pound of bruised currants and leave for another 24 hours. Repeat the straining and steeping with a third and final pound of currants the following day. Strain the vinegar into a measuring jug and for every pint (570ml) of juice add 12 oz (340g) of sugar. Boil the sugar and vinegar together for 10 minutes, then cool and bottle, et voilà, blackcurrant vinegar! You can add a few cloves and a stick or two of cinnamon when boiling if you prefer your vinegar spiced. The London Pharmacopoeia *of 1679 recommends just such a cordial as an excellent restorative: blackcurrants, both the leaves and the fruit, having long been looked on as a cure for everything from a sore throat to gout, diarrhoea and arthritis.*

Children will love the delicate flavour of fresh young leaves in Swiss roll or triangular shaped sandwiches: real one-up-personship when it comes to the gourmet lunch box? The leaves can be added to salads. They make a pleasant flavouring infused in milk puddings or they can be finely chopped and mixed into balls of cream or curd cheese—or plain tofu for that matter—for a dainty savoury.

6 oz (170g) sugar
¼ pint (140ml) water
1 handful of young, fresh, blackcurrant leaves
4 egg whites
juice of 1 lemon
¼ pint stiffly whipped double cream—optional

I use white sugar for this recipe because a white cream looks prettier. Boil the sugar and water with the fresh leaves for 15 minutes without stirring. (It is difficult to say what a 'handful' is and it doesn't really matter. This is a country recipe and exact measurements of some ingredients simply aren't necessary: your common sense will guide you!) Whisk the egg whites in a large bowl until they are stiff and peaky. The secret of whisking egg whites is to do it at a slow speed. Modern whisks are often too fast (even at their slowest speed) for the strings of the white to cope. They get tangled up instead of being gently pulled out to trap the air. If you feel your machine hasn't got a slow enough setting, use a hand whisk to begin, switching to an electric whisk once the whites are good and frothy. Quickly strain the hot syrup and pour it over the egg whites, whisking all the while. Continue to whisk until the mixture is really thick and creamy. Whisk in the lemon juice, and the whipped double cream if you are using it. If you are watching your fat intake, you could use fromage frais instead of double cream.

Serve the Blackcurrant Leaf Cream piled into glasses garnished with a couple of tiny leaves, and crisp biscuits. It makes a splendid dinner party sweet and can be prepared 24 hours in advance with no ill effects. In fact, without the cream, it will keep for up to 10 days in the fridge.

For a completely different flavour, substitute elder flowers for blackcurrant leaves. The flowers don't smell too good on the tree, but believe it or not, they taste wonderful.

Perfumed Crab Apple Jelly

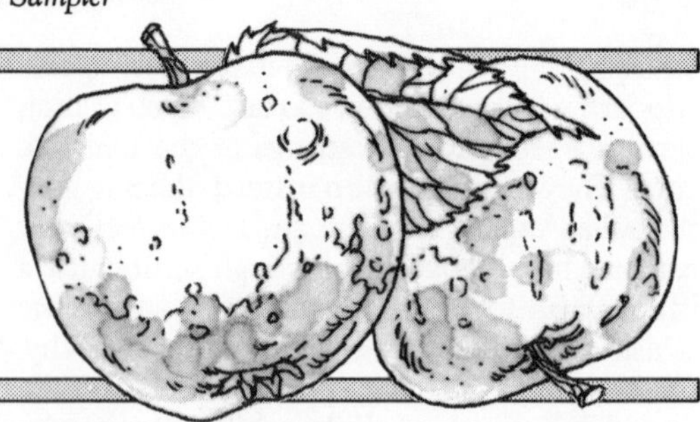

Crab apple jelly is one of those things that you either have never eaten or are sick to death of because you've had 200 pots and there's another 200 to get through before next season—there seems to be no in-between. For those who haven't tried crab apple jelly, let me assure you you have a treat in store. For those who have eaten too much and become bored with it, try adding some country flavourings to restore your interest. Crab apples, usually available in overwhelming abundance in later summer, don't have to be made into jelly. Pickled Crabs (doesn't that sound wonderful!) are delicious with any sort of vegetable burger, with strips of fried smoked tofu or, in the carnivorous household, with cold meats. To pickle crabs, bring a pint (570ml) of cider vinegar to the boil, add a stick of cinnamon, half a dozen cloves and a good teaspoon of pickling spices tied in an old handkerchief, and a pound (455g) of sugar. As soon as the sugar is dissolved, add a couple of pounds (about 1kg) of washed crabs (no need to peel them) and simmer gently until they are barely softened. Strain off the crabs, put them into hot, clean jars and boil the remaining syrup until it thickens slightly, then pour it over the crabs and cover the jars. A little fresh ginger at the bottom of the jars will add extra zip. Could anything be easier?

And now to the country flavours for plain crab apple jelly. When the jelly has been potted but is still hot, add a leaf or two of scented geranium (which must of course be clean). Lemon rose and the strongly-scented pineapple geraniums are all excellent.

Mint is another useful flavouring; just one tiny leaf of sage, verbena or lemon balm give still more variations, but use only a small amount for their flavours easily overwhelm. If you have scented roses growing in your garden, a handful or two, shredded and added four or five minutes before the jelly is finished boiling will really bring back the flavours of the past.

3 lb (1½kg) crab apples
1 pint (570ml) water
12 oz (340g) sugar to every pint of juice
any flavouring from the selection given

Wash the crabs—there's no need to peel them, just remove the stalks. Put them into a pan with the water and bring them to the boil. Simmer them slowly for about 20 minutes; they should be soft and broken but not pulped. Strain the whole lot through a jelly bag, preferably overnight. The simple country way was to suspend the bag on the legs of an up-turned stool, with a clean bowl beneath to catch the juice. Don't be tempted to squeeze the apples or your jelly will be cloudy. Measure the juice into a pan and for every pint add 12 oz (340g) of sugar. Boil rapidly for 15-20 minutes. Test the jelly for setting by dropping a teaspoonful onto a saucer. It it forms a skin, the jelly is ready. If it doesn't, allow a little extra boiling time. Pot into small jars and flavour as you will. If you are using rose petals, wash them well; you may need to pinch away the pale tip of each petal, where the petal was joined to the flower head. The tip is very bitter in modern varieties of scented roses, though not in the old ones. If in any doubt, pinch out the tip or your jelly may be ruined. Snip or tear the petals into shreds and add them for the last 5 minutes boiling. A little fresh angelica, instead of rose petals, is yet another option for flavouring, but scoop the stems out of the jelly before potting. The scented leaves mentioned in the introduction can be boiled with the jelly in just the same way if your prefer.

Borage Flower Soufflé Omelette

Borage grows like a weed once established in the garden. The flowers are so pretty, bright blue with an almost black centre, it seems a pity not to give them a little garden space. Culpeper himself recommended them as a tonic for those 'weak by long sickness' and the seeds as 'good to increase milk in women's breasts', while the roots and leaves 'cleanse and temper the blood'. John Evelyn prescribed borage to 'cheer the hard student' and 'revive the hypochondriac', while the ancient Greeks demanded a sprig in their wine for they believed it gave them courage. Perhaps our modern habit of adding a sprig of borage to Pimms or punch comes from this ancient belief. Given its myriad virtues, can you resist buying a packet of seeds? A lovely sixteenth century recipe from a Proper New Booke of Cokerye *gives a tart of borage flowers—mix borage flowers, 3 or 4 egg yolks, curd cheese and perhaps a little sugar and bake in a pastry shell. Hilda Leyel, of Culpeper fame, quotes a recipe by Robert May dated 1689 for candied borage flowers. The recipe recommends boiling the flowers in equal quantities of rose-water and sugar until they are candied. A perfectly good result can also be had by painting the flowers with lightly-beaten egg white, dipping them in caster sugar and drying them in a warm place before storing.*

This simple soufflé omelette of borage flowers is sprinkled with old-fashioned flavoured sugar before serving. Fill a jar with caster sugar and plunge the flavouring of your choice into the centre. Within a week you will have flavoured sugar. The longer you keep it, the more pronounced the flavour will be. Vanilla is the best known such flavouring. Store the pod you cook with in a jar of sugar to get double benefit. You can wash a used pod, dry it off and pop it back into the jar up to four or five times. A few sprigs of lavender or rosemary, a couple of bay leaves, a sprig of mint or a few scented rose petals are all old ways of making the most deliciously scented sugar for sprinkling or baking.

The quantities given are enough for one hungry person, or two with dainty appetites.

2 eggs
pinch salt
1 tablespoon water
1 teaspoon oil or butter
6–12 borage flowers
flavoured sugar for sprinkling

Separate the eggs and whisk the white with the salt until firm and peaky. Beat the egg yolks with the water until creamy, then fold them into the egg whites. Oil a pan, heat it and tip the mixture in. Cook, without stirring, over a moderate heat. Finish off the top under the grill, then sprinkle over the flowers and a little sugar. Fold the omelette in half and serve dredged with more sugar. A little crab apple jelly in the centre together with the flowers is a pleasant variation.

Savoury Tansy Pudding

Tansy is another very old country herb and, like marigolds, was a firm favourite with Reuben Truman in Still Glides the Stream. *He liked a few tansy flowers in his rice pudding, as well as a savoury tansy pudding that cannot have differed much from this recipe. Tansy has a long season, being amongst the first greenery of spring and lasting through until winter. No wonder the Greeks called it* Athanasie *or everlasting. Country folk placed a high value on the fresh green leaves after a winter diet of dried peas and beans and salted meat. John Evelyn, in his* Acetaria *(1699), rightly points out that tansy is a herb to be used with discretion,— a flavouring, rather than something to be added in handfuls. He suggests it be 'qualified' with other greens such as spinach or the leaves of primroses and violets. A mixture of such greens, fried and served with orange juice and sugar is, he says, 'one of the most agreeable of all boil'd herbaceous dishes'.*

There are many variations on tansy pudding, sometimes known as herb pudding, in old cookery books and manuscripts. They are usually based on bread or oats, the really old recipes using barley or groats (the kernels of oats). Almost any greenery would be chopped and added to the base, mixed with eggs, the fried or boiled as a pudding. The meat eaters amongst you could eat this tansy pudding with meat and veg. Vegetarians would serve it with steamed carrots, cauliflower and gravy, or, if the weather is mild, perhaps with a salad of chicory, beetroot and nasturtium flowers. Young borage leaves, gooseberry leaves, raspberry leaves, blackcurrant leaves, bistort, nettles or lady's mantle would all go into a herb pudding along with tansy, leeks, onions, chives or whatever else was growing in the garden.

Like all the country recipes there isn't really a recipe. It is more a matter of grasping the idea, then using what happens to be available.

1 lb (455g) spinach or mixed greenery
1 large onion
1 heaped teaspoon finely chopped tansy
4 oz (115g) fresh brown breadcrumbs
1 tablespoon oil or melted butter
2 hard-boiled eggs
1 fresh egg
½ pint (285ml) milk

Wash the greens and cook them with no added water. Peel and finely chop or grate the onion. Add the cooked, chopped greens (they should be quite dry), the onion and tansy to the fresh breadcrumbs. Stir in the oil or melted butter and the roughly chopped hard-boiled eggs. Beat the remaining egg into the milk and stir into the breadcrumb and greens mixture. Pour into a buttered pie dish and bake in a moderate oven, 350°F/180°C (gas mark 4), for 30–40 minutes. Serve as preferred. Leftovers are good sliced and fried in butter.

Vegans could omit the eggs, substitute soya milk or silken tofu for cows' milk and still have a perfectly acceptable pudding.

Elderberry Ketchup

There is, perhaps, no tree more shrouded in contradictory folklore than the elder. Gerard and Shakespeare were convinced that Judas Iscariot hanged himself on an elder tree, which is more than enough to give any tree a bad name! It's been called the Devil's tree and branches of elder have, since the earliest times, been symbols of disgrace and woe. Yet it was planted in virtually every cottage garden to keep witches away, and a quaint old Gloucestershire legend has it that elder wood is a certain cure for rheumatism. Culpeper swears by it for curing gout, piles, sore eyes, 'women's diseases', palsy, ulcers and all manner of other ailments, not to mention being an excellent black dye for hair. In northern Europe it is named after Hulda, the goddess of love to whom it is sacred.

Country dwellers, despite its mixed reputation, have long looked to the elder to stock their larders. We are all familiar with elderflower and elderberry wines, but in the past the shoots were pickled as a winter vegetable, while the flowers perfumed stored fruit and preserves. Elderberry chutney, syrup and ketchup would all be laid down for later consumption. A store of elderflower syrup makes cooling summer drinks and is the base for the most delicious water ice. It is also an excellent addition to any fresh fruit dish.

To make the syrup, collect enough flowers to fill a 2 pint (generous 1 litre) jug when gently pressed down, cover them with water and simmer the whole lot for half an hour. Leave it to steep, overnight if possible, then strain it. To every pint (570ml) of juice add 12 oz (340g) sugar and simmer for 10 minutes. A few cloves can be added to the pan if you like their flavour. All that remains is to bottle and store it for use as you please.

To make the chutney collect 3 lb (about 1½ kg) of ripe berries and boil them in 1 pint (570ml) of vinegar with ½ lb (225g) each of sultanas, onions and sugar and a teaspoonful each of cinnamon, allspice, cayenne and ginger and 4 oz (115g) salt. Simmer the whole lot together until you have a thick rich mixture. Bottle it, while still hot, in clean jars.

It has to be said, our foremothers knew how to go about the practical business of ensuring nature's bounty was preserved with minimum fuss and maximum benefit!

2 lb (900g) ripe elderberries
2 pints (1.2 litres) white vinegar
1 tablespoon peppercorns
1 teaspoon cloves
3 or 4 blades of mace
1 oz (30g) fresh ginger
1 large onion
2 tablespoons salt

Put the elderberries in a pan with the vinegar. Tie the spices in a piece of muslin—an old handkerchief is a useful, modern equivalent—and add them to the pan with the peeled and finely chopped onion and salt. Simmer for 25 minutes. Strain the liquor while still hot and bottle it.

In times past, this ketchup would have been used with fish or meat. For the modern vegetarian, it is a superb flavouring, and a useful vegetarian alternative to Worcester sauce (which contains anchovies) for soups and stews, or to add zest to virtually any savoury dish. Most bottled sauces contain a fair amount of undesirable additives and this home-made sauce is an excellent way of avoiding them.

Hazelnut Leaf Dolmades

Dolmades are of Turkish origin but, like so many foods, they are widely travelled. Of course they went first to Greece, as many a British tourist will know. In Cyprus they are known as Koupepia, and as variations on the theme the Cypriots also eat stuffed mangold leaves and stuffed courgette flowers. All are filled with rice flavoured with onions, parsley and mint, though in Turkey forcemeat is often preferred. Dolmades also travelled to Sweden, in 1715 to be precise, and became a national dish. The Swedes wrap their Kaldolmer in cabbage leaves, kal meaning cabbage, rather than vine leaves. They have a great Swedish warrior, King Charles XII, to thank for their Kaldolmer. After a campaign in Turkey, Charles returned to Sweden, hotly pursued by his Turkish creditors. It was the creditors' cooks who effected the transplanting of dolmades to Sweden. Since the Swedes had no qualms about using cabbage leaves or changing the filling from rice to minced veal, I have determined to feel no qualms about changing the filling back, and using an entirely different wrapping. I'm using young, tender hazelnut leaves for this dish. Just as hawthorn leaves are edible, so too are hazelnut leaves. You could also use very young, translucent beech leaves, but as they are small, they are especially time consuming to fill and roll. It is, I accept, something of a fiddle to make up a batch of tree leaf dolmades, but not very much more than using vine leaves. The effort is worthwhile as they are a delicious miniature nibble with drinks or a wholesome meal with salad. Despite a broad knowledge of cookery, I have never come across beech or hazelnut leaves used in this way. I have borrowed the idea from Danish nutritionist and cookery writer, Brigit Siesby. I can find no evidence of beech or hazelnut leaves in cookery being common anywhere in Scandinavia, though the trees are common enough in those northern climes. In Scandinavian folklore, the hazel tree was dedicated to Thor. Let's hope he won't mind us eating his tree!

30–40 hazelnut leaves
1 medium onion, peeled and finely chopped
2 cloves garlic
4 tablespoons oil
6 oz (170g) uncooked rice
3 oz (85g) pine nuts
1 teaspoon ground cinnamon
2 teaspoons dried mint
pinch ground cloves
juice of 1 lemon

Put the leaves in a large pan, cover with water and bring to the boil. Pour off the hot water immediately and cover the leaves with cold water until you are ready to use them. Fry the onion and garlic in 1 tablespoon of oil until soft and then add the rice, stirring well to coat each grain with oil. Add just enough water to cover the rice and cook it till all the moisture is absorbed and the rice is tender. Keep your eye on the rice as you may need to top up the water, but on no account drown it. Stir the rest of the ingredients into the hot, cooked rice, reserving only the lemon juice and the 3 tablespoons of oil as yet unused.

Now begins the part of the recipe that requires patience rather than skill. Put a good spoonful of mixture onto each leaf and roll it up neatly. Lay the filled leaves in a shallow dish, packing them closely together to avoid them unrolling. You could wedge any unfurling rolls shut with extra onion or garlic cloves. When you have used up all the leaves, mix the reserved oil with the lemon juice and a scant ¼ pint (140ml) of water and pour over the rolls. Cover with foil and bake in a moderately hot oven, 350°F/180°C (gas mark 4), for 1 hour. Serve hot or cold.

Index

Other recommended reading . . .

CORDON VERT

52 Vegetarian Gourmet Dinner Party Menus

Colin Spencer

Here are dinner parties for every week of the year, created by Britain's foremost newspaper columist on wholefood and vegetarian cooking. No corners have been cut in selecting the very best seasonal ingredients and the most luxurious and delicious items to produce meals which will be appreciated by everyone. The finest examples of international cuisine are represented, as well as many exciting and original dishes developed especially for this book. Vegetarian gourmets have found a kindred spirit in Colin Spencer, who firmly believes that none of the pleasures of dining need be lost simply because meat is not on the menu and presents a wealth of tempting recipes which amply prove his case.

CORDON VITESSE

Elegant Dinner Parties for the Vegetarian Host-in-a-Hurry

Cecilia Norman

Set the scene: the table is laid, the wine is on ice, subtle music is playing in the background, the guests arrive and everybody has a wonderful time – except, that is, for the cook, who has spent hours up to the elbows in flour, gets changed in ten minutes and then spends most of the evening in the kitchen away from the good company and lively conversation.

If this is the story of *your* dinner parties then help is at hand. Here are simple yet classy vegetarian receipes and menu ideas, designed for the busy cook. With the emphasis on high quality, gourmet foods, prepared with the minimum of fuss and time, it is easy to entertain in style without spending hours slaving over a hot stove.

Basic recipes are included for items to keep on hand in the fridge and freezer, with tips on time and labour saving techniques and devices. So now you can prepare delicious dinner parties with less haste and more speed.

Bon appetit!